HOW JESUS CHANGED THE WORLD

An ILLUSTRATED GUIDE to the UNDENIABLE INFLUENCE of CHRIST

CHRISTOPHER D. HUDSON

BARBOUR BOOKS
An Imprint of Barbour Publishing, Inc.

CONTENTS

Dedication

To Jesus

That may seem trite to some readers, but I can't help it.
He changed *my* world.

Acknowledgments

Creating a book like this requires many details to keep track of. Without my research and editorial teams, I would not have made it. Thank you to Barbara Leach. I'm indebted to you for sharing your insights and helping prepare some initial research.

Thank you to Mary Ann Davison, Nora Stoecker, and Robin Black for your fact checking and making sure everything in this book was accurate. And along those lines, thank you to Dr. Nathan Barnes for your thoughtful critique and review. You made this a much better book.

Thank you to Rich Murphy for helping me organize my notes and work early drafts. You were instrumental in helping craft this book. And special thanks to my editorial watchdogs: Robin Merrill, Alice Sullivan, and Mary Larsen.

Thank you to Karen Engle for your suggested improvements and insights. Thanks for helping organize the reviewers' comments and for the help with photo research.

Thank you to my friends at Barbour Publishing who helped cast a vision for this book. Can you believe we've been creating books together for nearly twenty years? Thank you for your ongoing trust and partnership.

How Jesus Changed the World

INTRODUCTION

In the history of the world, billions of people have lived and died, but most have not had much of a noticeable impact. Yet within each generation, a handful of people do impact the world and earn themselves a place in the history books.

Henry Ford is remembered for his transformation of modern industry. Alexander the Great and Napoleon are known for their military conquests. Martin Luther King Jr. is remembered as a great man who helped the world take steps to overcome prejudice and stereotypes.

While these great figures of history influenced the world in profound (but specific) ways, only one person has ever changed the course of history: Jesus Christ.

Jesus was born of a young virgin woman named Mary in the tiny and remote Israelite village of Bethlehem. But this baby born in obscurity has become a worldwide figure acknowledged by most of the world's religions. And though He last walked on the earth nearly two thousand years ago, His impact has shaped countless areas of history.

Christ nailed to the cross, Gerard David (c. 1460–1523)

The miracles Jesus performed—the people He healed, the people He set free from evil spirits, the dead He raised—stand as testimony to the anointing of God on His life and ministry. He truly came to do the work of the Father and not His own. Although He suffered and died, He also rose from the dead, something that no other religious leader can claim to have done.

Jesus walked on this earth for only thirty-three years. His active ministry lasted only three of those years; yet in that time, He put into motion events and teachings that would change the course of this world. The disciples He gained and the ministry He passed on to them has had a worldwide impact and is still having an impact today.

The chapters in this book outline specific historical events that occurred or were greatly influenced by the life and teachings of Jesus. The events include the following areas:

- Founding of hospitals
- Building of schools
- Increase of literacy
- Improvement of agricultural methods
- Expansion of the arts
- Advancement of architectural techniques
- Protection of women's and human rights
- Progress of exploration
- Development of science
- Maturation of economics
- Establishment of social agencies

How could all this be possible? How could a man who last walked the earth in AD 34 impact the economic development of the High Middle Ages? Because His teachings live eternally in the hearts and minds of the people He impacts. His influence has carried on through the work of those who have accepted Him as Lord and Savior. Each person has carried a little bit of Jesus with them, sharing Him with the world.

These people—from the famous writers to the unknown monks transcribing texts in some musty monastery—have all had their part in creating this story, the story of Christ's work here on earth. The story is not about them, even in the cases where we know their names. Rather, it is the story of Jesus, the Christ, lived out through the words and works of countless of His followers.

In an ideal world, Jesus and the church He commissioned would carry the same message and actions of love and grace. Unfortunately, history captures many ways the church has deviated from Jesus' teachings. The church led the way in some of the atrocities of the Crusades, built its power on the backs of poor people, and executed Christians during Salem's witch trials. While truly dark spots on human history, those actions were led by the church—not by Christ. As such, many of those subjects are not covered within this book. The purpose of this book is not to create yet another church history but to look at specific ways Jesus Himself has affected human history.

The goal in skipping over those moments is not to hide from the church's history or to pretend the church's influence has always been stellar; rather, it is to acknowledge that Jesus and the church are not one and the same. Jesus presented perfect humility and love. Throughout history, church leaders have wrestled with power and selfishness.

The church often does a poor job of showing Christ's love. This book will discuss some instances in a spirit of humble honesty. But this book is not anti-church. Yes, the church has led the way in some terrible practices, but the church has often self-corrected and realigned with the teachings of Christ—bringing Christ-inspired change, despite the church's shortcomings.

Christ by Rembrandt (1606–1669)

Many historical instances allow us to witness the teachings of Jesus carried by imperfect messengers. While the Spanish conquistadores were wrong to force Aztec Indians to convert to Christianity, the love and teachings of Jesus prevailed in the aftermath. The horrible circumstances with which the gospel arrived did not nullify its power. The message of Jesus is separate from the messenger.

AN INCOMPLETE STORY

This is not an exhaustive account of Jesus' effect on the world—that would take a library. This is simply an overview intended to shape thinking and encourage further discussion and research. Therefore, it was necessary to give certain topics only a quick mention or none at all.

It is hard to say where the world would be today without the life and work of Jesus. Clearly, it would be a much sadder world, with much more sin, sickness, and pain. Most of all, it would be a world without hope. Even in the darkest of times, even when Jesus has been misrepresented by the church, He has always brought hope. That hope, the hope of eternity in heaven, has been the inspiration for many, from the greatest to the least, who have all had one common trait—they followed Jesus and became part of His story.

Christopher D. Hudson
www.ReadEngageApply.com
Facebook.com/Christopher.D.Hudson.books
Twitter: @ReadEngageApply

Chapter 1
DEFINING THE FAITH
(AD 33–312)

On a hillside outside Jerusalem, eleven men stared intently at the sky. Moments before, they had listened to Jesus offer the final instructions of His earthly ministry. As He concluded His words, these dumbstruck disciples watched as He ascended to heaven in a cloud (Acts 1).

Stained glass of the ascension of Christ in the German Church, Stockholm, Sweden

Although Jesus' earthly ministry came to an end with His ascension into heaven, His influence on human history had only begun. The disciples Jesus left behind embodied His teaching and were emboldened by the Holy Spirit to fan the flame of Christianity. This new faith would change not only hearts but also the way people lived.

The significance of Christ has continued for over two thousand years, impacting nearly every aspect of life for believers all over the world. In the first century, Jesus' teachings and ministry influenced Judaism, challenged the Romans' view of the world, and made profound differences in the lives of people in Roman society.

> ## Jesus' Impact: The Great Commission
>
> "All authority in heaven and on earth has been given to me. Therefore go and make disciples of all nations, baptizing them in the name of the Father and of the Son and of the Holy Spirit, and teaching them to obey everything I have commanded you. And surely I am with you always, to the very end of the age." (Matthew 28:18–20)

INITIAL CHALLENGES TO JUDAISM

The first members of the Christian church—the three thousand who joined the church on the day of Pentecost—were almost entirely Jewish. These

A fresco of the first Pentecost from the Basilica del Carmine in Naples, Italy. Created in 1933 by Antonio Sebastiano Fasal

practicing Jews accepted Jesus as the long-awaited, promised Jewish Messiah. These initial believers probably did not think of themselves as joining a new religion but merely as embracing God's promise of a Messiah for the Jewish people as an affirmation of their strong Jewish faith.

The Hebrew community in Jerusalem was a broad tent that welcomed various sects within Judaism. Within the community were groups like the Sadducees (who did not believe in the resurrection of the dead), the Essenes (who adopted asceticism and daily baptism[1]), and the Zealots (who were known for embracing a hostile opposition to the Romans). While the inclusion of early Christians as another sect of Judaism may have caused stress for the Pharisees, who believed they had embraced a monopoly on pure doctrine, the addition of a new religious group may not have been as troubling for the community at large. These early Christ followers (called members of "the Way" in Acts 9:2) still attended the synagogue, worshipped at the temple, observed the Torah (the writings of Moses), and celebrated Jewish festivals. Several years into the first century, in Antioch, this group of believers was branded as "Christians."

The early Jewish Christians from Jerusalem attempted to maintain continuity between the Old Testament and the gospel of Jesus Christ. They embraced the idea that Christianity was simply a fulfillment of Jewish beliefs and a natural extension to God's story. The only difference between these believers and other Jews was that they accepted Jesus as the long-awaited Messiah. Other Christians outside Jerusalem quickly abandoned characteristic Jewish practices, such as a kosher diet and circumcision, which led to several attempts to reconcile Jewish and Gentile Christians.

This identification with Judaism helped the early church in profound ways. Because the Romans accepted Judaism as a local religion, Roman law protected Christianity's early practice and growth. The minor difference of whether the Messiah had come or was to come was inconsequential to the Roman rulers, although it was an item of hot contention among the Jews. As a result, the Romans left the

The earliest Christians identified themselves closely with Judaism.

earliest Christians undisturbed for the first years of the church. However, this protection was short-lived, and the Romans began persecuting the

Christians in the first century, coinciding with the Great Fire of Rome in AD 64.

How Jewish did the early followers of Christ consider themselves to be? Their convictions were strong enough that they questioned if it was possible for Gentiles to receive salvation. It took the strong and vocal leadership of Peter to open the door for Gentiles to become members of the church without adopting Jewish practices (Acts 10–11). As Paul began his ministry to Gentiles, tensions remained between Jewish believers and their new, non-Jewish counterparts. As a result, the apostles and elders of the church in Jerusalem convened in order to clarify God's plan of salvation for both Jews and Gentiles (Acts 15).

Paul considered himself to be the apostle to the Gentiles, and he brought the message of Christ to several major cities in the Roman Empire. Paul taught that Jews and Gentiles alike were in need of salvation by faith through grace—that the love of God brings healing and peace to both Jews and Gentiles if they have faith in God. Paul sought out those who desired to know God, regardless of their ethnic or religious backgrounds. He embraced every opportunity to teach them of the Jewish Messiah who offered salvation to all people.

Saint Paul, Claude Vignon (1593–1670)

As the number of Gentile believers grew, tension increased between Gentile and Jewish Christians. The words and ministry of Jesus—the gospel itself—became a defining concept for Gentile and Jewish people alike. Those who encountered Jesus would need to take a stand. Those of the Jewish faith who rejected Jesus began to define their orthodoxy in a way to exclude Christ, drawing a defining line between Judaism and Christianity.

Tensions and divisions continued to grow between the faiths, with Gentile Christianity gradually supplanting Jewish Christianity on the world stage.

Paul's Custom

Paul's custom was to go to the synagogue *first* upon entering a new town. Being a "tentmaker" and a Pharisee, Paul was often asked if he had any word to share with the Hebrew congregation (Acts 18:3–4). This was a common practice among the Hebrew people when an established teacher would visit. Paul took advantage of this custom to tell many congregations about Jesus.

Ruins of an ancient synagogue in Capernaum, Israel

SEPARATION FROM THE WORLD: HOW PAGANS VIEWED EARLY CHRISTIANS

Outside Israel, traditional Roman religion defined the Roman Empire. People across the land worshipped multiple gods and celebrated numerous festivals and ceremonies. Many of their practices focused on satisfying the flesh rather than on cultivating personal piety or caring for others.

When Paul traveled to Athens during his second missionary journey, he opened his message by commenting on the vast number of temples and

Jesus' Impact: Jewish Ties

"Do not think that I have come to abolish the Law or the Prophets; I have not come to abolish them but to fulfill them." (Matthew 5:17)

altars around the city. He acknowledged that the Athenians were so religious that they had built altars to every imaginable god. To cover their bases, they had even built an altar to an "unknown" god to avoid offending any of the gods they may have forgotten. This acknowledgment of an "unknown" god

The Parthenon in Athens, Greece

became Paul's segue to teach them about the one true God, the Creator of heaven and earth (Acts 17:22–24).

Christians began to stand out from the rest of the population because of their constant absence from these pagan festivals and ceremonies. Because these religious practices were a vital part of a city's social life, the Christians' nonattendance became apparent, setting them apart from normal society. Christians were living out the words of Jesus: "[My followers] are not of the world, even as I am not of it" (John 17:16). At the same time, their neighbors developed rumors about these peculiar people, accusing them of immoral living and even cannibalism. Suspicion grew into fear, which quickly led to persecution.

But why were Christians seen as different? Jesus' teaching changed and challenged the hearts of His followers in a way that would affect their words, attitudes, and actions. His teaching on personal holiness emphasized actions that came from a genuine heart and faith (Mark 7:20–22). Because traditional Roman practices often conflicted with Christian sensibilities, Christians alienated themselves from the fabric of Roman life, leaving them vulnerable to scapegoating and persecution.

> ## Jesus' Impact: Being Different
>
> "What comes out of a person is what defiles them. For it is from within, out of a person's heart, that evil thoughts come—sexual immorality, theft, murder, adultery, greed, malice, deceit, lewdness, envy, slander, arrogance and folly." (Mark 7:20–22)

OTHERWORLDLINESS

Early Christians and pagan Romans differed in how their faith impacted daily life. While pagans might have engaged in fertility rites or paid homage to a god in hopes of improving their earthly lives, early Christians focused instead on a future world. Convinced that Jesus' return was imminent, these early Christians kept their hearts pointed heavenward, awaiting the promise of being reunited with Jesus, either on earth or in heaven.

Many Christians showed exceptional courage in the way they responded to their persecutors. Numerous ancient writings discussed how poor and suffering Christians still praised their God regardless of their difficult earthly life. Some nonbelievers simply could not understand how Christians could be indifferent about their suffering. As Justin Martyr (AD

Peter's crucifixion illustrated the words of Justin Martyr: "Death is a debt which must at all events be paid." *Image:* The Crucifixion of St. Peter *by Caravaggio (1571–1610)*

100–165) put it, "Death is a debt which must at all events be paid" (*The First Apology of Justin Martyr*). Christians lived with a hope of the next life in heaven.

John, the beloved disciple of Jesus, stated: "Do not love the world or anything in the world. If anyone loves the world, love for the Father is not in them" (1 John 2:15). Several stories of Christian martyrdom reveal how persecuted followers of Christ took this teaching to heart as they "set [their] minds on things above, not on earthly things" (Colossians 3:2). While many early believers firmly established this new way of life as the norm, the rest of the world watched with incredulity.

Jesus' Impact: True Life

"For whoever wants to save their life will lose it, but whoever loses their life for me will find it." (Matthew 16:25)

An early Christian letter attempted to preserve the laudable characteristics of early Christian living: "They live in their own countries, but only as aliens. They have a share in everything as citizens, but endure everything as foreigners. . . . They obey the established laws, but in their own lives they go far beyond what the laws require." The writer of this letter, who had clearly seen that Christians were living a different sort of lifestyle, also stated, "It is true that they are 'in the flesh,' but they do not live 'according to the flesh.'"

While Jews separated themselves from society, Christians also did so, but in different ways. Jews celebrated their religious observances, which were clearly identifiable by those around them. However, the practices of Christians seemed less formal and less ritualistic than those of their Jewish counterparts. This made Christians appear strange to the pagan people around them and also began to set them apart from traditional Jews.

It wasn't long before Christianity stood apart from Judaism. This "new" group was actively evangelizing and adding to their ranks quickly. As the numbers of Christians began to grow, they found themselves at odds with Roman leaders, who preferred the consistency and stability found in a society that practiced traditional forms of paganism.

CARE FOR THE POOR

Widows, orphans, and the poor posed significant problems for the Roman Empire. The poor fended for themselves by engaging in prostitution, selling themselves into slavery, living on the streets, or finding other desperate means to support themselves.

However, poor, sick, and homeless neighbors provided Christians with a practical way to apply the teachings of Jesus—to love one another as He had loved them (Matthew 5:44; John 13:34–35). This others-centric behavior stood in stark distinction to that of the people around them.

With unique concern for the young, some Christians brought orphaned children into their homes, a practice virtually unheard of in the day. (Roman families also brought orphaned children into their homes but with the intent to enslave them.) This care for needy children distinguished Christians from other people who would routinely abandon unhealthy or unwanted infants. When pagans practiced infanticide, Christians of-

Jesus' Impact: Caring for the Poor

"For I was hungry and you gave me something to eat, I was thirsty and you gave me something to drink, I was a stranger and you invited me in, I needed clothes and you clothed me, I was sick and you looked after me, I was in prison and you came to visit me." (Matthew 25:35–36)

ten rescued those left to die, bringing helpless children into their homes and giving life to those condemned to die or languish in slavery.

While orphans were a favorite charity of early Christians, the church also cared for the poor in general. Christians buried the dead of those whose families couldn't afford to do so, regardless of their faith or background. These early Christ followers also provided food for the poor. In Antioch, it is believed that the church regularly fed as many as three thousand of the city's poor.

The pagan neighbors of the Christians couldn't help but notice this outpouring of love and care to the poor. One satirist named Lucian (c. AD 120–180) wrote, "The earnestness with which the people of this religion help one another in their need is incredible. They spare themselves nothing for this end. Their first lawgiver put it in their heads that they were brethren." Even pagans were eventually encouraged by their leaders to follow the Christian lead in this. Julian the Apostate (c. AD 331/332–363) furthered this cause by saying, "Nothing has contributed so much to the progress of the superstition of the Christians as their charity to strangers."

While done with great love, helping those in need came at a high cost, often both socially and financially. The great theologian Clement (c. AD 150–215) captured the attitude of the early believers by saying, "He impoverishes himself out of love, so that he is certain he may never overlook a brother in need, especially if he knows he can bear poverty better than his brother. He likewise

A Fresco of St. Clement from the Cathedral of Aarhus (Denmark)

considers the pain of another as his own pain. And if he suffers any hardship because of having given out of his own poverty, he does not complain."

This willingness to suffer in order to help others added credibility to the Christians' message of the cross, opening people's hearts to realize that Christianity was not an empty religion. It was new in the earth, not just in its form and beliefs, but in the fact that its adherents were willing to suffer daily, if suffering helped them to express love for others.

The idea of suffering in order to show love to others became pervasive throughout the early church. Many ancient church writings note not only the willingness of Christians to help but also their willingness to suffer in order to do so. The *Apology of Aristides* is typical of surviving Christian literature: "And if there is among them any that is poor and needy, and if they have no spare food, they fast two or three days in order to supply to the needy their lack of food."

The love of Jesus became evident through the example of early Christians, who reached out to society's poor and eventually influenced the world at large to care for the needy.

First words of the *Apology of Aristides* written in Syriac, a widespread language in the first century

EQUALITY BETWEEN RICH AND POOR

Both Roman and Jewish society propagated a rough caste system. The rich benefited; the poor suffered. Each segment of society knew and abided in their place. While it was possible to move from one caste to another, it was rare due to innate prejudices and economic realities. The teaching of Jesus and the early church sometimes defied these societal norms. James, the brother of Jesus, said:

My brothers and sisters, believers in our glorious Lord Jesus Christ must not show favoritism. Suppose a man comes into your meeting wearing a gold ring and fine clothes, and a poor man in filthy old clothes also comes in. If you show special attention to the man wearing fine clothes and say, "Here's a good seat for you," but say to the poor man, "You stand there" or "Sit on the floor by my feet," have you not discriminated among yourselves and become judges with evil thoughts? Listen, my dear brothers and sisters: Has not God chosen those who are poor in the eyes of the world to be rich in faith and to inherit the kingdom he promised those who love him? But you have dishonored the poor. . . .

If you really keep the royal law found in Scripture, "Love your neighbor as yourself," you are doing right. But if you show favoritism, you sin and are convicted by the law as lawbreakers. (James 2:1–9)

There was no equivalent to the modern-day middle class during New Testament times. Although there may have been different levels of wealth, usually people fell into one category or the other: rich or poor. The poor vastly outnumbered the rich, with artisans, craftspeople, farmers, widows, and slaves all relegated to this lower social class. One-third of the population may have been slaves under Roman rule, with some estimates raising that number to over half of Rome's population.

Slavery existed from the earliest times of world history, and the economy of the Roman Empire relied on it. While masters owned their slaves, treatment

This second-century mosaic captures an image of slaves serving their masters.

of slaves varied extensively. Some owners treated slaves well, educating them and giving them responsibility. Others treated slaves harshly and as disposable property. In fact, many gladiators were slaves whose owners donated them to the games.

Slaves lacked freedom and autonomy, but it was in the masters' best interest to treat them with some level of dignity. Over time, some slaves were given great responsibility by their owners. Some managed their owners' business affairs. Others were set free after a period of time. Church history shows that some former slaves held positions of authority and leadership within the church, even rising to the position of bishop. One slave eventually became a pope.

CALISTVS ·I· PP· ROMANVS

Nineteenth-century depiction of Pope Calixtus *Image:* from The Lives and Times of the Popes *by Chevalier Artaud de Montor, originally published in 1842.*

Pope Calixtus I was the bishop of Rome from approximately AD 218 until his death, circa AD 223. While not referred to as "pope" during that time period (as the term had not yet been coined), the Roman Catholic Church has since bestowed that title on him. In his earlier years, Calixtus was a slave who worked for a Christian owner. He later decreed that a Christian slave could marry a free person and receive the church's blessing, regardless of what Roman law said. He ran away in fear because he had lost some funds placed in his care but was later recaptured and sent to work in the mines. After a period of time, he was transferred to Rome along with some other Christian slaves (at the request of the emperor's mistress, who was said to be a Christian). Once set free of the mines, he went to work for the bishop of Rome, whom he later followed as bishop.

Allowing the poor and slaves to hold positions of importance flew in the face of Jewish and Roman practices. In both cultures, as in many ancient societies, poverty was considered a curse and wealth a divine blessing. Slowly but surely, the treatment of the oppressed by the church as it applied the teaching of Christ began to influence perspectives.

Christianity was the first religion to challenge the traditional practices of slavery. In his writings, Bishop Ignatius (c. AD 35/50–98/117) discussed that while the early church could not do away with slavery entirely, early Christians would purchase slaves in the marketplace for the sole purpose of setting them free. Even Christians

The apostle Paul wrote: "There is neither Jew nor Gentile, neither slave nor free, nor is there male and female, for you are all one in Christ Jesus" (Galatians 3:28).

who owned slaves were admonished in Paul's writings to treat their slaves differently—to treat them as brothers rather than as slaves (Philemon 15–16).

The matter was so important to the apostles Peter and Paul that they each taught about the right treatment of slaves, as well as the proper way for slaves to act toward their masters (Ephesians 6:5–9; Colossians 4:1; 1 Peter 2:18–21). Neither condemned slavery but rather treated it as a neutral institution in society. Like Christ, they focused on the internal heart of a slave and an owner instead of on their positions in society. These early church leaders reminded Christians that all people are born as slaves to sin and their spiritual state matters more than their earthly position.

A great example is Paul's epistle to Philemon, which is an entreaty on the part of Paul that Philemon receive back Onesimus, a runaway slave. But Paul wouldn't be satisfied with Philemon accepting Onesimus back as a mere slave; he insisted that the slave be welcomed back as a brother. Going further, Paul offered to pay any offense and debt incurred by Onesimus's absence—a great act of love on behalf of a slave (Philemon 17–18). How could Paul offer to pay the debt of a runaway slave? Paul was a firm believer that all people are created equal and made equal in their faith: "There is neither Jew nor Gentile, neither slave nor free, nor is there male and female, for you are all one in Christ Jesus" (Galatians 3:28).

Building on Paul's teachings, the early church theologian Clement wrote, "Slaves are men like ourselves." Nearly a century later, another great Christian writer, Lactantius (AD 240–320), wrote, "Slaves are not slaves to us; we deem them brothers after the spirit, in religion, fellow-servants."

Though Jesus Himself never addressed slavery, the absence of this subject in His teachings reminds us that His primary mission and concern focused on the heart of humanity. His determination was to rescue people into the kingdom of God and to have their hearts settled there, rather than work to better their worldly positions with riches or status.

Jesus remained steadfastly focused on His mission during His earthly ministry. To criticize Jesus for not confronting slavery reveals an ignorance of Jesus' ministry and superimposes a different set of values on His ministry objectives. Jesus' mission was to bring salvation to humanity, not evoke social change.

The heart of Jesus' teaching, which urged the respect of human life and love for one another, eventually helped the church influence slavery in Rome. Eventually, a number of church leaders came out boldly against slavery, condemning it and calling for slave owners to emancipate their slaves voluntarily. Other leaders followed the example of Peter and Paul, calling for masters to treat their slaves well and slaves to obey their masters and work hard for them.

Many slaves were emancipated during the reign of Constantine the Great in the fourth century.

While Rome never eliminated slavery during this time period, the manner of slave ownership changed. The growing Christian worldview helped shape a culture that eliminated slave cruelty and gave some rights to the slaves. Roman emperor Constantine (c. AD 272–337) passed a law banning the branding of slaves on the face, and in AD 325 he banned the gladiator games (though they continued into the sixth century). Other laws gave slaves increased rights.

More than anything, church leaders influenced society to treat slaves as equal brothers and sisters in the faith. Within the church, slaves found equality, enjoyed the sacraments, and participated in church activities.

CHRISTIAN PRACTICE OF COMMUNAL SHARING

With hearts set on a heavenly kingdom rather than an earthly one, some early Christians lived communally with one another. Some sold and shared property, some earned money, and everyone worked to meet the needs of others. Unlike Communism, which emerged almost 1,900 years later, Christian communal living was voluntary. Meeting each person's needs in a loving way was the goal, not redistribution. Acts 4:34–37 reflects this practice:

> There were no needy persons among them. For from time to time those who owned land or houses sold them, brought the money from the sales and put it at the apostles' feet, and it was distributed to anyone who had need. Joseph, a Levite from Cyprus, whom the apostles called Barnabas (which means "son of encouragement"), sold a field he owned and brought the money and put it at the apostles' feet.

This behavior of living was not directly taught by Christ (at least not in the teaching recorded in the New Testament), but Jesus and His disciples modeled this sort of lifestyle as the disciples

Mosaic of Justin Martyr as it appears in the Church of the Beatitudes near Capernaum (Israel)

Christ and the Samaritan Woman by Angelica Kauffman (1741–1807)

traveled for three years with expenses being paid by one purse (John 12:6). And though communal living may not have been one of Jesus' key topics in teaching, it is one application the early church emphasized as believers made an effort to show selfless love toward all by putting others' needs ahead of their own. Along these lines, Justin Martyr wrote to Emperor Antoninus Pius (AD 86–161), "Before we loved money and possessions more than anything, but now we share what we have and to everyone who is in need."

BREAKDOWN OF CULTURAL BARRIERS

Christianity broke traditional cultural barriers. Regardless of race, nationality, culture, or class, all people were invited to the cross of Christ. Once members of the family of God, Christians accepted their new brothers and sisters as equal peers in the sight of God.

Generally speaking, the ancient Romans, Greeks, and Jews didn't discrimi nate against others based on race, but they did draw strict cultural lines. In all three cases, a person was either part of them or an outsider. Jews have always referred to these outsiders as Gentiles, while both Greeks and Romans referred to everyone else as barbarians.

All the people groups that Rome conquered were forced to accept the language of Rome and pay tribute, and urged to embrace its culture. Those who became Romanized by taking on their customs and speech were treated better than the others, even though they were still conquered people. The difference was merely in whether they had adopted Roman culture.

As a gospel for all people, Christianity set itself apart from all other religions. It was culturally and ethnically diverse, with members from all walks of life and all ethnic groups. The message of salvation was available to all people, regardless of culture and background. When the early Jewish Christians had trouble accepting this truth, the Holy Spirit revealed to Peter that the message of salvation was for all people (Acts 10). The church opened its doors to everyone.

Jesus modeled this acceptance of all races and peoples in His ministry. He received people from all cultures, even those whom the Jews typically avoided. When He healed the Roman centurion's servant (Matthew 8:5–13), He showed love for His cultural suppressor. When He showed kindness to the Samaritan woman (John 4:5–26), He demonstrated great love for the social outcast.

> **Jesus' Impact: Love for All People**
>
> "My command is this: Love each other as I have loved you."
> (John 15:12)

The life and teaching of Jesus inspired Christians to cross cultural lines. Christ welcomed anyone who followed Him into His family and into citizenship in heaven (Matthew 12:50). While members of the early church still lived within Roman boundaries, they had become primarily citizens of heaven. The new culture of all believers was the culture of the kingdom of God, not that of Rome.

The kingdom of God has no place for bigotry, with its citizens being called to live in unity. Where prejudice exists, unity cannot. There are three arguments in scripture, all of which are central to the Christian faith, that speak out strongly against any justification for prejudice:

- We have all come from a common ancestor; therefore, we are all brothers and sisters in the same family (Romans 4:16–17; Galatians 3:16, 26–29).

- Salvation is freely given to all who accept it, regardless of their background or current state in life (Romans 3:22; 1 Corinthians 12:13).
- At the end of all things, all humankind will face the same judgment before the same throne and be judged based on the same criteria. There will be no favoritism as we stand before that throne (Romans 14:10–12).

This is not to say that there were no differences between people in the church. Each was an individual, and all came from different races and cultures. The early church recognized those differences, and its members made an active effort to accept all who came, regardless of their race and culture. As each learned to exemplify Christ's love, they would adapt one to the other by making the necessary compromises in behaviors—but not in their faith—so that all could fit in.

Justin Martyr wrote, "There is not one single race of men whether barbarians or Greeks, or whatever they may be called, nomads, or vagrants, or herdsmen living in tents, among whom prayers and giving of thanks are not offered through the name of the crucified Jesus" (*Dialogue with Trypho*). Ultimately, the common ground for all who call themselves by the name of Christ is Jesus and His sacrifice on the cross. In that, all are equal and all remain equal, regardless of whatever else they may be.

A life-size representation of Diana. This marble statue is thought to be a Roman copy of a Greek statue attributed to an artist named Leochares (c. 325 BC).

EFFECTS ON IDOLATRY

The pagan Roman religions emphasized idolatry. Each deity was represented by its own figure and house of worship. Followers built huge, expensive temples, and artisans made miniature copies for the people to take home and put in prominent places.

Judaism first—and then Christianity—broke the mold by condemning idolatry in all its forms. God's Ten Commandments outlawed idolatry,

Ruins of the ancient city of Ephesus

and the early church maintained this teaching of Judaism in condemning idolatry of any form. In doing so, they made enemies with local residents and with the artisans who made their living by creating those idols.

When Paul visited Ephesus, his teaching stifled the sale of idols (Acts 19). Demetrius, a silversmith, gathered together his fellow craftsmen and raised a near riot over Paul's teaching. (It is interesting to note that Demetrius and the men with him weren't concerned as much about any point of religious doctrine as they were over the potential loss of income.) While the mob took on the appearance of being driven by ideology, it was Demetrius's speech about their loss of business that incited these people to anger. The combination of a loss of income and a loss of prestige in their city was more than they were willing to bear, and they created civil unrest.

While the love of money is a powerful vice, capable of swaying hearts and inciting anger, Christians in the early church saw through the duplicity of a pagan religion that was largely based on profit and offered genuine faith to those who would receive it. Having had an encounter with the living God, these Christians would not bow their knee to a piece of stone or wood. Nor could they make an image of their God, the ruler of heaven and earth.

Within a couple of centuries, Christianity continued to increase in membership by so much that the pagan temples fell into disrepair and many forms of idolatry largely passed away.

CARE OF THE SICK

The Roman world faced disaster in the third century with the arrival of a great plague that blanketed the empire. And although the general population reacted with understandable fear, Christians stood out during what turned out to be one of the defining moments of the new faith.

> **Jesus' Impact:**
> **Compassion for the Sick**
>
> When he saw the crowds, he had compassion on them, because they were harassed and helpless, like sheep without a shepherd. (Matthew 9:36)

The Plague of Cyprian arrived in the Roman Empire, probably via sailors and traders who were contagious, having contracted it either in the Middle East or Africa. Firsthand accounts from the time period describe a deadly disease that could cause diarrhea and vomiting, bleeding eyes, decaying limbs (that would sometimes fall off), and damage to hearing and sight. (Many historians speculate that this plague was smallpox.[2] The plague affected the empire from AD 250 to 270.)

The plague spread rapidly, killing thousands. (Estimates range from 300,000 deaths to upward of 500,000.) Crowded city life, primitive sanitation, and lack of medical knowledge made it easy for the disease to spread.

Pagan priests, doctors, government leaders, and other residents fearfully fled the cities in an effort to avoid catching the plague. Left behind in the cities were the poor, sick, elderly, and dying. Christians once again faced an opportunity to practice Jesus' teachings about loving and caring for others.

In many cities across the empire, Christians became the prime caregivers for the sick. While they recognized that they were not immune to the plague, they were confident that this world was not their ultimate destination (John 14:1–3). This confidence gave them the faith they needed to face the plague and care for the sick. Christians offered words of explanation and comfort in a situation where nobody else offered solace. Their acts of mercy helped position Christianity as a faith based on love and attract survivors to join their ranks.

Around AD 260, a writer named Dionysius summed up the Christian attitude in his writing by stating:

> Most of our brother Christians showed unbounded love and loyalty, never sparing themselves and thinking only of one another. Heedless of danger, they took charge of the sick, attending to their every need and ministering to them in Christ, and with them departed this life serenely happy; for they were infected by others with the disease, drawing on themselves the sickness of their neighbors and cheerfully accepting their pains. Many, in nursing and curing others, transferred their death to themselves and died in their stead.

The Christians' response to the plague and their care for the sick drew an unprecedented amount of respect and admiration from many pagan worshippers, who turned to Christianity during this period.

This sudden increase in numbers and growing admiration for Christianity also came with backlash. Emperor Decius blamed the plague on the Christians and their effort to turn Roman citizens away from Roman religion. Although

This is a painting of Sergius and Bacchus. Both men were fourth-century Roman soldiers who were martyred for their faith in Jesus Christ.

Christ Heals the Paralytic, Bartolomé Esteban Murillo (1617–1682)

he initiated new persecutions to scare believers into turning away from the church, his efforts did not slow the growth of the Christian faith or stifle the efforts of Christians who cared for the sick. When Christians nursed sick pagans back to health, many of the formerly sick became followers of Jesus. In addition, these new believers who were healed acquired a natural immunity to the plague, which allowed them to fervently minister to the needs of the sick without any fear of becoming afflicted once again.

While believers were officially under persecution, the people of Rome admired and respected them for their dedication and loving service to all. Tertullian (c. AD 160–220) summarized the feelings of many when he wrote the following about his fellow Christians: "It is our care for the helpless, our practice of loving-kindness that brands us in the eyes of many of our opponents. 'Only look,' they say, 'look how they love one another.'"

WILLINGNESS TO SUFFER FOR RIGHTEOUSNESS

Heavy persecution continued to mark the church through the first three centuries. The nature of the persecution was sporadic, depending on the political atmosphere in each region. Still, as Christianity grew, many in the Roman leadership felt that the Christian faith was a growing threat to the empire. They were especially troubled by a lack of loyalty by Christians, who claimed respect for Caesar but declared they served another—the King of all kings.

The Christian Martyrs' Last Prayer, Jean-Léon Gérôme (1824–1904)

During this period, Christians suffered persecution from the central government in Rome for 136 years. The persecution varied at a regional level based on the local leaders and the level of respect the population had for Christians. This gradually tapered off toward the end, but during much of that time, many Christians were forced to choose between martyrdom and a renouncement of their faith. Few chose the path of renunciation, earning them much respect from the people and anger from their persecutors.

The early Christians saw martyrdom as something to be accepted—or even sought—rather than something to avoid. They were willing to suffer in this life, knowing that their suffering would lead to joy in the next life. They were confident in God's ability to carry them through that suffering and give them the grace to stand strong until the end. Earthly suffering was of little consequence to people who kept their eyes fixed on heaven. Whatever might happen to them was merely temporal, with no eternal weight.

Enraged by the Christians' strong will, many of the Roman emperors sought ways to force Christians to abandon their faith. They pronounced edicts making Christianity illegal, stole Christian lands, removed believers in Jesus from public office, and specified severe punishment for those who insisted on following Christ. While some of these edicts required proof of illegal activity, many did not; they declared that worshipping Jesus was enough to make one guilty. Because of their blatant refusal to deny God, many of the most famous early church theologians and apologists died as martyrs during this time.

As most people are naturally afraid of death, the Christian willingness to face it with a song on their lips was incomprehensible to outsiders. As Stark states in *The Rise of Christianity*, "The bravery and steadfastness of the martyrs was proof of Christian virtue. Indeed, many pagans were deeply impressed."[3] Since people aren't usually willing to die for a lie, the willing acceptance of Christians to die for their faith stood as a strong statement of what they preached.

Pressure to renounce Christ did little to change Christians' minds, which frustrated government officials. Instead, the faith of the Christians as they faced death became one of the greatest evangelistic tools the church had available to it. Gary Habermas and Michael Licona point out in their book *The Case for the Resurrection of Jesus* that the disciples

> were radically transformed to the point that they were willing to endure imprisonment, sufferings, and even martyrdom. This indicates

1700° ANNIVERSARIO DELL'EDITTO DI MILANO

Oratorio di San Silvestro, Roma - Basilica dei Santi Quattro Coronati

EMISSIONE CONGIUNTA ITALIA - CITTÀ DEL VATICANO

This postage stamp was printed in Italy in 2013 to commemorate the 1,700th anniversary of the Edict of Milan.

that their claim of seeing the risen Jesus was the result of a strong and sincere belief that they truly had seen him.[4]

Much to the Roman government's dismay, persecution didn't slow the growth of Christianity but likely had the opposite effect. Some Christians were led to their death, which empowered other Christians to embrace the same fate while pagans watched with curiosity. Other Christians escaped local persecution by traveling to other parts of the empire, bringing their message of salvation with them. With Christianity growing, it became impossible for Roman officials to wipe it out. In some areas, Christians may have even become the majority of the population, outnumbering the pagan population. The faith of the believers, as well as the simplicity of the gospel message, appealed to many.

Sporadic persecution continued until Emperor Constantine, who ruled the West, and Emperor Licinius (c. AD 250–325), who ruled the East, issued the Edict of Milan in AD 313. The edict granted Christians legal standing in the Roman Empire.

Some historians have speculated that since Emperor Constantine found himself ruling a nation with a growing Christian faith and a declining Roman paganism, his conversion was nothing more than a calculated political decision. Regardless of his motives, Constantine's pronouncement for Christ changed the history of the church and of Rome. Over time, Rome became a Christian nation, with the church and the state firmly wedded together. It stayed this way for several centuries. Yet as the church grew in numbers, influence, and power, it began to wane in genuine devotion of believers and piety.

**Jesus' Impact:
The World's Reaction**

"The world cannot hate you, but it hates me because I testify that its works are evil." (John 7:7)

SEXUAL MORES

In pre-Christian Rome, the worship and celebration of all things in excess was commonplace. And as Roman citizens became wealthier, they also became more decadent in every way. It was within this sexually charged society that the church was founded.

The church stood in contrast to the Roman culture, where adultery, homosexuality, and pedophilia were commonplace. Even the theater used young boys to play the roles of women and pushed them to engage in homosexual behavior in order to portray their roles more convincingly.

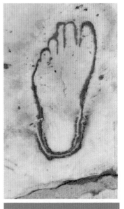

Romans viewed sexual acts as mere physical gratification without any true spiritual or emotional value to it. Temple prostitution was common, and the sexual acts performed with religious prostitutes were promoted as "love offerings" to the gods.

This footprint etched in marble advertised a brothel in ancient Ephesus.

Chastity in marriage was not the norm. Slaves, prostitutes, and children were exploited in extramarital affairs. Because slaves were property, masters expected them to perform sexual acts. Prostitutes were legal. These convenient liaisons offered an outlet for depraved behavior without fear of retribution or relational requirements. In a real sense, having sex with a slave, prostitute, or child eliminated the relationship problems associated with sex in marriage or the trouble that might occur from seducing a neighbor's wife.

Roman temple in use between 500 BC and AD 300. This temple is located on the island of Sardinia.

IMPACT ON ABORTION AND INFANTICIDE

Due to the low value placed on human life in general, the Romans (along with many other ancient people) easily disposed of unwanted children. Despite the dangers, they at times practiced abortion. Due to primitive medical practices, many women died due to abortions. Many others who survived the procedure suffered infertility. The resulting sterilization added to the decline of the Roman population.

Roman custom allowed a husband to demand that his wife abort or, more likely, abandon an unwanted baby. While abandonment of babies of both sexes occurred, parents abandoned baby girls more readily than baby boys. Extramarital affairs were commonplace, yet a pregnancy resulting from an affair caused embarrassment to a married woman. Many women felt it was easier to have an abortion than to go through the pregnancy and then abandon the unwanted child. This uninhibited sexual lifestyle also

> ### Jesus' Impact: Sexual Perspective
>
> "Haven't you read," [Jesus] replied, "that at the beginning the Creator 'made them male and female,' and said, 'For this reason a man will leave his father and mother and be united to his wife, and the two will become one flesh'?" (Matthew 19:4–5)

led to a rise in abortion among prostitutes and those who found themselves pregnant and needing to return to their work.

Poor Romans perceived babies as financial burdens. Those at the top of the social and economic ladder saw them as inconveniences. Both attitudes slowed the growth in the general population. Meanwhile, Jewish and Christian populations grew more rapidly.

The difference of attitude between Christians and their contemporaries was captured in the Epistle of Mathetes to Diognetus: "They beget children; but they do not destroy their offspring. They have a common table, but not a common bed. They are in the flesh, but they do not live after the flesh. They pass their days on earth, but they are citizens of heaven."

Christians went further than just voicing their opposition to the killing of babies by embracing abandoned children as their own. This charitable lifestyle saved the lives of many children who otherwise would have died of dehydration, exposure, or wild animals. The lives that held no value to the pagan Romans held incredible value to the Christians, who saw the same spark of God-given life in these children that they saw in their own.

With the Christians' habit of rescuing unwanted children—as well as their refusal to expose their own children—Christian families continued to grow in size and influence. As a result, the overall number of Christians in society began to outpace non-Christians.

Individual Christian leaders openly opposed the popular exposure practices of Rome, and by the end of the fourth century, the Christian voice was unified. The Council of Ancyra in AD 314 prescribed ten years of penance to any woman who had an abortion.

The Canons of Saint Basil, written in the fourth century, explicitly opposed abortion. Basil (AD 330–379) also organized public protests against abortion. More than just providing opposition, he also organized the first help for pregnant women with unwanted pregnancies. This work by Basil came to the attention of Emperor Valentinian (AD 321–375), bringing the contrast of Roman and Christian views on infanticide before him. Confronted by the Christian attitude, Valentinian acted by outlawing infanticide in AD 374. This law didn't eliminate the problem overnight, because many couples continued the practice in secret. However, the church continued to stand against abortion and infanticide, passing a number of canons opposing them.

The church was founded in the midst of all this debauchery and sin. Christian and Jewish attitudes about sex greatly contrasted with the sexual immorality of the pagan Romans. Christians viewed sex as an expression of love and respect between a married couple. Sexual contact outside the bonds of matrimony was strictly forbidden. Jesus' teaching forbids lust, let alone extramarital liaisons; He taught that sexual intimacy has the purpose of binding the couple together as one flesh (Mark 10:7–9).

The book of Hebrews, written within the early church time period, sums up the early church's attitude about sex very well: "Marriage should be honored by all, and the marriage bed kept pure, for God will judge the adulterer and all the sexually immoral" (13:4). Hundreds

The Mass of St. Basil, Pierre Hubert Subleyras (1699–1749)

of years later, under the influence of Augustine (AD 354–430), the church turned a corner and began to have a negative attitude about sex.

Christians rescued abandoned infants and also opposed abortion because they saw all children as unique creatures made in the image of God Himself. As such, to kill an unborn fetus is and has been considered murder in the eyes of the church. Even in that time, members of the church called women who induced abortions murderesses.

The opposition to abortion likely created larger families for Christians and a safe haven for pregnant women who did not want to discard their children. The larger families and attractive, pro-family atmosphere soon became an unintended recruiting tool for the early church—one more reason the early church began to grow and draw members from disillusioned pagan neighbors.

Saint Augustine in Prayer, Sandro Botticelli (1445–1510)

Naturally, these Christian attitudes offended some Romans who took the Christians' high view of life as a condemning judgment. Still, their moral conduct amazed many. A Greek physician named Galen (c. AD 250–325) said of the Christians, "So far advanced in self-discipline and. . .intense desire to attain moral excellence that they are in no way inferior to true philosophers."

As Christianity grew and its influence spread, so did biblical teaching about the sanctity of life, the purpose of sexual intimacy, and the importance of living a moral life, bounded by self-control. Eventually, the Christian attitude about these things became the norm in the Roman Empire, displacing the pagan practices that were in place at the time of the church's birth.

QUESTIONS

1. Why didn't early Christians see themselves as starting a new religion?

2. In what ways did the lifestyle of early Christians become attractive to some pagans?

3. How did the Christians' hope for a new world cause them to live differently in this world?

4. Why was the Plague of Cyprian a turning point of Christianity?

5. How did Jesus' teaching on sexual behavior influence the church?

Chapter 2

THE IMPACT OF JESUS ON RELIGION, POLITICS, AND CULTURE
(AD 313–600)

When Jesus taught on the grassy hills of Galilee, He said, "No one can serve two masters" (Matthew 6:24). Jesus knew that His followers could not commit to Him if their hearts also pursued money, position, or power. In fact, Jesus condemned those who focused solely on earthly power and admonished His followers to serve with humility, without regard to their position. The leaders of the early church era found themselves in a conflict between two masters. The church began to be swallowed up by power and its pitfalls—a problem that has plagued the church since that time.

Hillside in Galilee

As the church moved into the fourth century, its position, influence, and power began to change. Christians had lived under heavy persecution for over two hundred years, and suddenly the state lifted the oppression. Christians no longer had to hide their faith but were able to openly worship. Soon the majority of the empire's population identified themselves as Christians.

During this time, Constantine (c. AD 272–337), the first Christian Roman emperor, declared himself in support of the church of Jesus Christ. This event changed history, as the lines of power quickly blurred between the church and the state.

Constantine's Conversion

While there are those who say that Constantine accepted Christ, there are also a large number who are not so quick to accept that claim. This latter group sees Constantine as one who co-opted the church in order to benefit from it. He covered all the bases, hoping to find the favor of God, just as he sought the favor of other gods.

Mausoleum of the Roman emperor Galerius, now the Church of the Rotunda and a UNESCO World Heritage Site

Emperor Constantine ascended to the throne with the most powerful days of the Roman Empire behind him. The sprawling empire proved difficult to govern. Enemies threatened from all sides, weakening Rome's hold on some of its farthest frontiers. Birth rates in the empire declined, and lawless behavior grew more common.

One year before Constantine became emperor, his predecessor, Emperor Galerius (c. AD 260–311), signed the Edict of Toleration in AD 311. This ended the last great Roman persecution of Christians, and it granted official permission to worship God the Father and Jesus Christ openly.

Because the state had tried unsuccessfully to eradicate Christianity for two hundred years, this policy shift aimed to co-opt Christianity and bring believers into good standing with the empire. Rather than fight Christianity, the edict offered protections already due other faiths and insisted that Christians pray for the welfare of the Roman republic.

The edict aligned with Jesus' teaching to "give back to Caesar what is Caesar's" (Mark 12:17). Jesus and the early church had admonished Christians to submit to the government and to give them respect and honor (Romans 13:7). The Roman government's request for Christian subjects to pray for Caesar found a readily receptive audience that could now pray for Caesar publicly and openly.

Two short years later, in AD 313, Constantine issued the Edict of Milan. This pronouncement confirmed the earlier statement of the Edict of Toleration and added provisions for church property to be returned to the Christians. This edict made specific provisions for Christianity and also renewed the earlier request that Christians pray for the republic.

The Edict of Milan began a marriage relationship between the empire and the church, which evolved into an interdependent relationship. It also brought the emperor into the church as the church's protector and patron. From this point onward, Constantine built basilicas and exempted the church from paying taxes (a similar arrangement was enjoyed by paganism in the empire).

> **Jesus' Impact:**
> **Submission to Government**
>
> Then Jesus said to them, "Give back to Caesar what is Caesar's and to God what is God's." (Mark 12:17)

Statue of Constantine the Great, the leader who changed the relationship between church and state

Whether due to Constantine's genuine faith or merely his political expediency, Jesus' followers would change the Roman Empire. This change affected the course of the world's history.

Although Christianity had survived—even thrived—under Roman persecution, differing factions emerged because individual leaders governed unique congregations. Across the empire, differences in theology and biblical interpretation spurred varying opinions and ways of teaching. As Christianity became legal, the church needed unity in thought.

The relationship between the church and the state brought about many other changes as well. What started as mere toleration quickly gave way to Christianity's rise as the predominant religion of Rome. By AD 324, Constantine had moved from toleration of all religions to becoming openly hostile toward the pagans. This change of policy broke from Roman tradition, which had endorsed the worship of pagan gods since its inception.

Constantine favored Christianity and occasionally made it difficult for pagans to practice their religion. He also sought to unify the church by attacking outlying Christian groups who disagreed with the church in Rome. The majority of the church considered splinter groups, such as the Arians (who believed that Jesus did not always coexist as part of the Trinity but was created by God the Father), to be heretics. These groups came under state censure.

The Council of Ancyra (AD 314), a regional ecumenical council of bishops in the area of modern-day Turkey, denounced worship of Artemis, a goddess widely revered in their area. They also dealt with believers in

The Context of Constantine

Less than ten years before Constantine began his rule, Emperor Diocletian made a final Roman attempt to stamp out Christianity. He outlawed the faith, ordered that copies of the scriptures be burned, and initiated wide-spread persecution. Church historian Eusebius wrote about this time in his *Ecclesiastical History*:

That they should be maimed by burning the sinews of the ankles of their left feet, and that their right eyes with the eyelids and pupils should first be cut out, and then destroyed by hot irons to the very roots. And he then sent them to the mines in the province to endure hardships with severe toil and suffering.

This was the world when Constantine rose to power.

Sculpture of Artemis, original artist unknown

the church who had failed in their duty to Christ due to persecution. When necessary, the church removed some Christians from the fellowship of believers and disciplined others.

As time went on, Christianity grew and other religions became outlawed. However, the government's new zeal to protect the Christian faith began to cause the church to lose sight of Jesus' teaching. Rather than follow Jesus' mandate of love, the church and state persecuted other faiths as cruelly as Christians had been persecuted in the previous century. The Roman state robbed the treasuries of pagan temples and closed Jewish synagogues.

By AD 380, Christianity had transformed the empire. Emperor Theodosius I (AD 347–395) accepted baptism and declared Rome to be a Christian empire. For the first time, a ruler submitted himself to the church and gave the clergy—especially Ambrose, the bishop of Milan—incredible power and authority.

Bishop Ambrose (c. AD 340–397) served as both a spiritual and political adviser to the emperor. Rome appointed him the consular prefect (similar to a modern-day governor) of Liguria and Emilia, two provinces in modern-day northern Italy, which he controlled from Milan. This position gave him secular power to go along with the spiritual authority he wielded. Ambrose enjoyed more than regional civic authority; he also influenced the emperor.

Jesus' Impact:
The Kingdom of God

Jesus said, "My kingdom is not of this world. If it were, my servants would fight to prevent my arrest by the Jewish leaders. But now my kingdom is from another place." (John 18:36)

On one occasion, Bishop Ambrose used his influence to affect public worship in Rome. During the reign of Emperor Valentinian II (AD 371–392), some pagans petitioned to

Painting by artist Camillo Procaccini (1551–1629): Saint Ambrose prevents Emperor Theodosius I from entering the basilica after the Massacre at Thessaloniki (in 390).

have an altar restored outside the Roman Senate House. Symmachus, the prefect of Rome at this time, sided with the pagans and submitted his own request to Valentinian in favor of restoring the pagan altar (known as the Altar of Victory). Ambrose wrote Valentinian as well, warning him about supporting superstition and threatening to censure him if the emperor rebuilt the altar. The fear of the church's action persuaded Valentinian to deny Symmachus's request.

Whether by accident or design, Ambrose developed the formula that allowed the church to control Rome for the next several centuries. While the emperor reigned supremely, the church usurped an even higher position. Church leaders could always hold the sword of censure or excommunication over the heads of secular rulers, forcing Roman emperors to act as the church saw fit.

As the church grew in earthly power, its leaders lost sight of Jesus' teachings that pointed to the kingdom of heaven, which reminded followers that His kingdom was not of this world.

IMPACT ON THEOLOGY

Eastern Orthodox icon depicting the First Council of Nicaea of 325, led by Constantine

Three hundred years after His earthly ministry, Jesus' character, identity, and teaching became a public debate. Constantine realized the need to help define orthodoxy: Who was Jesus? What did He teach? What happened on the cross? Answering these questions became a significant task during this period of the church.

The more the church grew, the more it suffered from disagreements over theology. In its earliest days, the original disciples managed to maintain the purity of doctrine. Paul's writing often dealt with various false ideas and heretical teachings. At one point, the apostles formed a council to make determinations about doctrine (Acts 15). But once persecution drove early Christians from Israel, the church lost its central authority to settle disputes over differences of interpretation or beliefs.

In the days before the printing press, both the handwritten copies of the Bible and oral traditions were prey to unorthodox teachings.

In AD 325, Constantine undertook the work of unifying the church by convening the Nicene Council. He invited the bishops of all the Christian churches to join and rally behind a gospel message. Church leaders discussed at length the relationship between Jesus and the Father. The council evaluated three differing viewpoints:

Christ Created	One Essence	Similar Substance
Christ was created by God the Father and was of a different substance. This viewpoint was furthered by Arius (AD 250/256–336), along with the Egyptian bishops Theonas and Secundas.	Christ was one in essence and substance with the Father. Hosius of Cordova (c. AD 256–359) and Athanasius (c. 296/298–373) championed this more orthodox position.	Christ was of a similar substance with the Father. This belief distrusted the term *homoousios* (of the same substance) because it had been misused to say that the Father and Son were one and the same. This viewpoint, represented by Eusebius of Caesarea (AD 260/265–339/340), was doctrinally closer to the more orthodox viewpoint.

In the end, the position of Hosius of Cordova and Athanasius prevailed and became the orthodox viewpoint as the bishops came into agreement over it. The church declared Arius heretical and disallowed his teaching in the church. While Christ's essence dominates the historical accounts of this session, the council yielded other vital outcomes. The group discussed other doctrinal issues, defined the structure and government of the church, and outlined the responsibilities of the clergy. Another historic conclusion from the synod established the celebration of Easter on the first Sunday occurring after the first full moon after the March equinox.

The members of the council wrote out their conclusions as a series of canons or laws. Together the group created a single statement of faith, which aimed to unify all churches and provide a means of teaching the people the basic principles of Christianity. The resulting statement (known as the Nicene Creed) became a universal declaration of faith. This creed later expanded, in 381, into the Nicene-Constantinopolitan Creed, which stands to this day.

The creed consists of two distinct sections. The first section discusses the doctrine of the Trinity—that salvation comes from the acceptance of a triune God. The second section reaffirms Jesus as fully divine and also fully human.

Original Nicene Creed of 325	The Nicene-Constantinopolitan Creed of 381 (popularly known today as the Nicene Creed)
We believe in one God, the Father almighty, maker of all things, visible and invisible;	We believe in one God, the Father Almighty, Maker of heaven and earth, and of all things visible and invisible;
And in one Lord Jesus Christ, the Son of God, begotten from the Father, only-begotten, that is, from the essence of the Father, God from God, light from light, true God from true God, begotten not made, of one essence with the Father, through Whom all things came into being, things in heaven and things on earth, Who because of us men and because of our salvation came down and became incarnate, becoming man, suffered and rose again on the third day, ascended to the heavens, and will come again to judge the living and the dead;	And in one Lord Jesus Christ, the Son of God, the Only-begotten, Begotten of the Father before all ages, Light of Light, Very God of Very God, Begotten, not made; of one essence with the Father, by whom all things were made:
And in the Holy Spirit.	Who for us men and for our salvation came down from heaven, and was incarnate of the Holy Spirit and the Virgin Mary, and was made man;
	And was crucified also for us under Pontius Pilate, and suffered and was buried;
	And the third day He rose again, according to the Scriptures;
	And ascended into heaven, and sits at the right hand of the Father;
	And He shall come again with glory to judge the living and the dead, Whose kingdom shall have no end.
	And we believe in the Holy Spirit, the Lord, and Giver of Life, Who proceeds from the Father, Who with the Father and the Son together is worshiped and glorified, Who spoke by the Prophets;
	And we believe in one, holy, catholic, and apostolic Church.
	We acknowledge one Baptism for the remission of sins.
	We look for the Resurrection of the dead,
	And the Life of the age to come. Amen.

A piece of the Rylands Papyri from the sixth century AD, believed to be the oldest extant copy of the Nicene Creed

EFFECTS ON POLITICS AND THE GOVERNMENT

Regardless of perceived progress, the church and state swallowed each other, as much as Jesus would have had it otherwise. By becoming embroiled in politics, the leaders of the church abandoned the leadership of Jesus. While He never taught that believers shouldn't be involved in politics, He made it clear that a Christian's heart should be focused on the kingdom of heaven. Although the teaching of Jesus influenced the government of the early Middle Ages, the lure of power dragged the church away from faithfulness to Christ.

When Emperor Constantine made Christianity acceptable in the Roman Empire (AD 313), he took ownership for the government of the church. He also sought the advice of the church's leaders in governing the empire.

Church and state grew so closely wedded that some people simultaneously held influential positions in both the church and state governments. While he left the decisions about spiritual manners in the hands of the bishops, Constantine integrated himself into the operation of the church authority and structure.

The church seemed to enjoy new prosperity and may have relished its ability to overcome Christ's warning to His followers: "You will be hated by everyone because of me" (Matthew 10:22). Not only was the church loved, it was embraced by the state and achieved a position of power. But in accepting this new position, the church left behind the core teaching of Jesus that said the world would hate believers because they did not belong in this world. With the state and church intersecting at many levels, Christians settled comfortably into the world—the very thing Jesus warned against. Ironically, the advances of the church into the mainstream of power caused Christians

Mosaic of Emperor Constantine presenting a model of Rome to the Virgin Mary (Hagia Sophia, Istanbul, Turkey)

to forsake Jesus' core teaching (John 15:19).

While the church supposedly kept to spiritual things, the spiritual realm was commonly understood to be part of everyday life. Therefore, the church would be expected to intervene in all areas of life and government.

At the same time that the church and state grew intertwined, the state itself was going through great turmoil. Constantine reunified the divided kingdom after overcoming Emperor Licinius in AD 324, but then moved his capital from the city of Rome far to the East, to what came to be known as Constantinople. This eventually led to the kingdom dividing once again, as it was

The extent of Constantine's empire

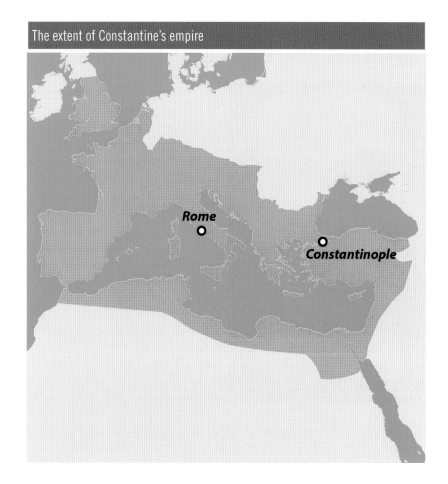

difficult to maintain communications with the lands in the western part of the Roman Empire.

This communication difficulty left the western part of the empire without clear guidance. The government was rarely seen. In response, many transferred their allegiance to the pope, who had remained in Rome. With no other governmental representation, the pope ended up directing many civil affairs by default.

THE EMPEROR CONSTANTINE

Although Constantine became the benefactor of the church, there's no way to know if he really embraced Christ. History can show us a person's actions, but it can't tell us the inner workings of a person's heart. It is quite possible that he straddled the fence his whole life, never taking that step across into the kingdom of God.

Early in his reign, during October of 312, Constantine and his political rival, Maxentius, met in battle at the Milvian Bridge, an important route over the Tiber River. It is told in a legend that before the battle, Constantine set aside time to pray. During his reflection, he considered the inadequate results emperors had garnered in praying to the pagan gods of Rome. To achieve success, he wanted the favor of one who could provide him with genuine help. This desire led him to begin praying to the God of Christianity.

Marble bust of Maxentius created between AD 306 and 312, artist unknown

As Constantine prayed, he saw the vision of a Chi-Rho cross above the sun. Along with the cross, he saw the words "By this symbol, you will conquer." According to legend, many others saw the vision as well. As he pondered the meaning of what he saw, Christ appeared to him with the Chi-Rho and told him to make the likeness of this symbol and use it as a standard against his

The Chi-Rho symbol on a panel from a Roman sarcophagus (AD 350), illustrating the resurrection of Christ

enemies. Constantine called together craftsmen and put them to work making the symbol and painting it on the Romans' shields.

There are several problems with this legend, starting with a high probability that the believers of the time would have taken this emphasis on a symbol as a form of idolatry. They would most likely not have accepted Constantine's vision or its interpretation, despite his position as emperor.

Nevertheless, Constantine won a major military battle. He began to spend a great deal of time with Christians thereafter. He learned about their beliefs, ate with them as equals, and regularly joined their discussions. During these discussions, he would send his guards outside, symbolically stripping himself of rank and position.

Constantine cared passionately for unity in the church. His discussions with Christians focused on finding common ground and agreement. Still, doubt remained about his conversion. While he participated with Christians in their celebrations, he also paid public honor to the sun god, Sol Invictus, whom he had served his whole life.

It is a strong possibility that Constantine truly converted to Christianity and genuinely followed Christ. Because the Christian church grew in power, he gained their support by becoming part of them. It is also a strong possibility that Constantine feigned conversion for political reasons. Like a good politician, he gave himself options with the people he governed by maintaining both Christian and pagan connections. Even after his supposed conversion, many of his actions remained purely pagan. These actions likely expressed his own beliefs, allowed for political opportunity, or revealed a lack of proper biblical knowledge.

Late in life, Constantine requested baptism as a Christian (AD 337). The church regularly offered an end-of-life baptism as a common practice for those of the Christian faith, even those previously baptized. Baptism helped Christians prepare for death, and Constantine's baptism followed these practices. Whether he genuinely converted or not, Constantine impacted the church and advanced the teaching and ministry of Jesus.

IMPACT ON PAGAN RELIGION

Whether real or politically expedient, Constantine's conversion brought many benefits to the church. While Christianity wasn't elevated to the

Constantine's Conversion, Peter Paul Rubens (1577–1640)

official religion of Rome until almost seven decades later, Constantine often behaved as if Rome existed as a Christian nation.

Bishops and priests performed the function of imperial advisers, both at the national and local levels. In exchange, clergy received tax exemptions for their service to the community. Money from the state treasury built and rebuilt churches, including cathedrals and big basilicas, as well as funded those churches. Under the reign of Constantine, the operating budget of the church grew larger than the expenses of the imperial civil service.

Constantine escalated his involvement in church government, convening ecumenical meetings and encouraging the development of creeds. He rebuilt Jerusalem, which weakened the Jewish influence in Israel. While no formal persecution of the Jews existed, they felt pressured like everyone else to convert to Christianity. Jews viewed this change in culture and its accompanying behavior as the first Christian persecution of Judaism.

The rise of Christianity wasn't without a steep price. The church, fully integrated with the Roman government in a symbiotic relationship, assumed the trappings of a Roman establishment. This amalgamation caused the Romanization of different facets of the church—including its artwork, which depicted Jesus and the disciples as looking more Roman.

While the Roman church worked hard to retain doctrinal orthodoxy, it was not immune to the influences that infiltrated it under Constantine's rule. Just as the Roman government had previously controlled the pagan religions, Constantine influenced Christianity, and leaders of the church accepted his leadership in exchange for his protection. Although this decision had negative consequences, Christian leaders embraced the change as they stepped out of a life of persecution and into imperial favor. Their imperfect environment came with newfound freedoms.

The pagans, however, found life much harder under the popularity of Christianity. Constantine and his successors continued to create edicts that led to the persecution of pagans and the confiscation of treasures from pagan temples, which were delivered to the church.

THEODOSIVS
Der Kevser

Then in 380, Theodosius made Nicene Christianity the official religion of Rome, outlawing paganism and all other religions. The Eastern Orthodox Church, Oriental Orthodoxy, and the Catholic Church each claim to be the historical continuation of this church in its original form. While this edict spurred church growth, it did not guarantee the genuine commitment of new believers—fear never does. The state and church's pressure on pagans to

Roman emperor Theodosius I was the last emperor to rule over both the eastern and the western parts of the Roman Empire.

Roman emperors Julian, Jovian, Valens, Gratian, Valentinian I, and Theodosius I (fourteenth century AD)

convert led to many new apparent converts who secretly maintained their pagan beliefs and practices. Since government leaders awarded civil positions only to Christians, many likely feigned conversion simply for personal gain. As expected, conversions based on personal gain only weakened the church, most especially in the areas of personal piety, discipline, and self-sacrifice.

After Theodosius abruptly retired, Valentinian I took over as emperor. Valentinian's sons Valentinian II and Gratian (c. AD 359–383), both of whom succeeded their father on the throne, continued to persecute pagans and support the church. While Constantine himself acted in large part as the head of the church, Gratian refused the title of Pontifex Maximus (chief bridge builder); for the first time, that title was passed on to the Catholic pope.

> **Jesus' Impact:**
> **Turning from Pagan Worship**
>
> "And when you pray, do not keep on babbling like pagans, for they think they will be heard because of their many words." (Matthew 6:7)

The Julian Calendar

The Roman calendar, established by Julius Caesar in 46 BC, created a way of keeping time using the months January through December. This Julian calendar (named in Julius Caesar's honor) was a solar calendar, which befitted a nation that worshipped the sun. In contrast, the Jewish calendar that God established was based on the lunar cycle. When the Julian calendar was modified to start in the year of Christ's birth, it remained a solar calendar.

Our calendars provide one of the most obvious ways that Jesus changed the world. In ancient centuries, historians and authors counted years in terms of a king's reign. (Haggai 1:1: "In the second year of King Darius. . .") Within a few centuries of Christ's birth, the world recast time into counting the years before or after His birth.

A Scythian monk named Dionysius Exiguus (c. AD 470–544) revised the calendar based on the birth of Jesus. In AD 525 he calculated the date of Jesus' birth, based on Luke 3:1 and 3:23. His calculations, though some scholars believe are inaccurate, set Jesus' ministry starting at the age of thirty, in the fifteenth year of the reign of Tiberius Caesar. As the reign of Tiberius began in AD 14, Dionysius calculated Jesus' birth at year zero.

Dionysius had a number of motivations for changing the calendar. First, Rome counted the years based on Emperor Diocletian (c. AD 245–311). Because Diocletian severely persecuted Christians, Dionysius sought to reboot the calendar with a different point of origin. Second, the pope had asked him to assign the dates of Easter for the next few years. Third, Dionysius's change to the calendar sought to eliminate fear of the world nearing its end. During this time, people superstitiously believed that the world would end 500 years after the birth of Christ. Dionysius's calendar revealed that Jesus' birth occurred 525 years before, which laid that panic to rest.

Seventeenth-century astronomer Johannes Kepler discovered that Dionysius had made an error in his calculations. According to Kepler's calculations, Jesus' birth occurred in either 4 or 5 BC.

Jesus' Impact: God's Calendar

"Heaven and earth will pass away, but my words will never pass away." (Matthew 24:35)

Monks in Kepler's day hesitated to study chronologies because they held time as God's singular affair. Finally, Pope Gregory XIII (AD

Illustration of Johannes Kepler, who contradicted Dionysius's calculations on the birth of Christ

1502–1585) established the reform of the calendar in 1582, which led the new calendar to be named in his honor. As this change came after the Christian Reformation and the weakening of the Catholic church, it took time for people to accept the Gregorian calendar. It became fully adopted by the eighteenth century.

IMPACT ON RELIGIOUS HOLIDAYS

Woodcut from the seventeenth century of Pope Gregory XIII by artist E. Hulsius

Throughout most of history, holidays served as special days with religious significance. Christianity developed its own calendar of these holy days as well. It only makes sense that a Christian society would create a series of holidays that would honor Christ and provide teaching opportunities to propagate the faith.

Christian holidays weren't frivolous occasions meant for getting together to have a party or enjoying a day off work. These people of faith established religious celebrations for the purpose of worshipping God and teaching church members about important events. (Our word *holiday* comes from the Middle Age English shortening of *holy day*.) This emphasis on a day of religious significance differs from many purely festive holidays celebrated in modern times.

Along with a natural connectivity with Judaism, the earliest church continued to celebrate the holidays that stemmed from the Hebrew calendar. These festivals and celebrations commemorated what God did for the nation of Israel, but they began to lose their meaning as more and more Gentile Christians joined the church. Christians slowly disconnected from their Jewish roots and instituted holidays that focused on Christ and His work. Naturally, remembrances of Christ's birth and passion moved to the forefront, becoming times

The Age of Augustus, Jean-Léon Gérôme (1824–1904). This painting depicts the birth of Christ with a clear Roman influence.

of holy celebration long before any official church calendar came into existence. Because of the importance of Christ's work on the cross, Jesus' death and resurrection remained the most important celebration and focus of the church year.

The act of remembering these events developed into the celebration of Holy Week. This coincides with the Jewish holy day of Passover and the weeklong celebration known as the Feast of Unleavened Bread. In this case, at least, the Jewish holiday and the Christian one coincided.

The Roman state officially sanctioned the celebration of Christ's birth on December 25 in the year 336. While there are records of Nativity celebrations before this date, they weren't consistent or clearly established as a church holiday.

The selection and establishment of December 25 allowed the celebration of Christmas to replace the pagan holiday that celebrated the winter solstice. The choice of this day also allowed for the celebration of Christ's circumcision eight days later on January 1.

ASSUMPTION OF SECULAR OR PAGAN HOLIDAYS

In recent years, many bloggers have complained that the church under Rome adopted the holidays and customs of pagans as their own holidays. While often true, the context of these decisions explains the rationale and can remove some of the negative connotations associated with these decisions.

Although Rome had made it illegal to worship pagan gods, the practical task of converting people's faith was not as easy as commanding it. By redefining known holidays, the church redeemed them for their own purposes. This replacement approach made it easier for new Christians to adapt to their new religion.

Jesus' birth as depicted in a painting displayed in Milan, Italy

The celebration of Christmas (the Christ-mass or mass of Christ) provides the greatest example of this. Many ancient religions celebrated the midwinter solstice in one manner or another. Some cultures even declared that the sun would disappear if their worship didn't turn the path of the sun on that exact date.

While Roman paganism wasn't quite that extreme, it did celebrate the victory of the sun god and light over darkness at the winter solstice. The ancient pagans believed that the Unconquerable Sun (Sol Invictus) was born on that date. Choosing this day for the celebration of Christ's birth allowed the church to usurp the pagan festival of the Unconquerable Sun held on the winter solstice.

Roman Celebration of Death

People of Roman times did not celebrate birthdays as we do today. Rather than celebrate births, the people of ancient Rome remembered the deaths of loved ones. As such, Roman Christians remembered and esteemed Jesus' death before the church developed regular Christmas celebrations.

To that end, the church did indeed commandeer the pagan Roman holiday to institute Christmas. Its action allowed an easier transition for pagans who converted to Christianity, and it provided the church with an opportunity to teach about the birth of Christ—the One who overcame darkness and lives within us.

The early church similarly replaced New Year's Day. Before Christ, the pagans celebrated the New Year with a drunken celebration that indulged physical passions. The church replaced this debauchery with the Feast of the Circumcision—a day to remember the circumcision of Christ when He was eight days old. By modern logic and counting, eight days after Christmas would occur on January 2, but the people used the same method of counting as the earliest church did. In the case of Easter, the Gospel writers claimed Jesus was buried for three days, even though He was dead only part of Friday night and Sunday morning. By similar counting techniques, January 1 lands eight days after December 25.

Easter eggs, one of many Christian traditions with pagan roots

A sparkling Christmas tree—which some believe to be of pagan origin—in front of a New York City church

In addition, the church likely redeemed symbols used as part of these various pagan celebrations. While we'll never know the actual origin of the Christmas tree, many legendary stories reference how the Christmas tree replaced a similar pagan symbol. One traditional story recounts that Saint Boniface (c. AD 675–754) chopped down an oak tree used by pagans. After his defiant act, he found a fir tree growing at the base of the oak tree and used its triangular shape to exalt the Trinity.

> **Jesus' Impact:**
> **The Power of Jesus' Words**
>
> "I am the way and the truth and the life. No one comes to the Father except through me." (John 14:6)

IMPACT ON THE WORKWEEK

Jesus' resurrection on a Sunday affected the standard workweek we still know today. The church recognized Sunday as a special day and a reminder of

Christ's resurrection. Today most of the global church continues to worship each Sunday in honor of Christ's resurrection.

The differences between the Sunday Sabbath of Christianity and the Jewish roots of a Saturday Sabbath are found in Old Testament and New Testament scripture. As far back as the Exodus, scripture shows God commanding that the people of Israel reserve the seventh day, the last day of the week, as a holy day to commemorate the last day of the creation week, on which God rested. No work was allowed, and they worshipped God on that day.

In contrast, we find Christians gathering together on the first day of the week as early as the book of Acts (Acts 20:7). Symbolically, this change in priorities puts the worship of God before any other activity in a week.

Constantine made this Sabbath change an edict of Rome in AD 321, known as his Sunday Law. It closed all places of business on Sundays, creating the first day of the week as an official day of rest. However, the law allowed those working in agriculture to work, as the animals and fields needed care. Later Roman laws and church canons built upon Constantine's Sunday Law, reserving Sunday as a day of rest and worship.

Jesus' Impact: True Worship

"For the Son of Man is Lord of the Sabbath." (Matthew 12:8)

IMPACT ON ENTERTAINMENT

Jesus taught about holiness, the sanctity of life, and the importance of loving others in all areas of life. Because of His teachings, the lasting influence of Christ changed entertainment as Christians gained influence in Roman society.

In the early centuries of the church, Roman citizens enjoyed many forms of entertainment, including the Olympics, the Isthmian games, poetry, and oratory competitions.

Two forms of entertainment that stood at odds with Christian morality were the gladiator games and the theater. The gladiator games, which focused on death, included battles between gladiators as well as other events that led up to the grand finale. In a day of games, the state publicly executed criminals and killed animals. Gladiators entered the arena in a wild spectacle. The sponsor of the games (usually a high-ranking politician) sat in a prominent position and sought favor from the masses.

Because the Roman culture did not value the sanctity of life, the people enjoyed watching the deaths of convicts, conquered soldiers, and animals. The games fed the crowd's desire for entertainment and satisfied their bloodlust. These games grew to become a normal, acceptable part of life.

Christianity and the teachings of Christ stood in opposition to this aspect of popular culture. Not only had Jesus taught that murder was wrong, but He raised the standard by saying that violent attitudes toward others equaled

the severity of murder (Matthew 5:21–22). He also emphasized that God specially and intentionally created humanity and, as such, humans possessed a high value (Matthew 6:25–6:34). The church treasured human life; therefore, Christian leaders condemned the gladiator games because of the needless gore and celebration of the loss of life. Over time, Christian efforts to apply the teaching of Jesus began to change the entertainment and bloodlust culture that had survived for hundreds of years.

The Roman Colosseum, the largest amphitheater in the Roman world, where gladiators fought

Fifth-century Byzantine mosaic depicting gladiator games

As the church and state unified in many areas, Christian morality slowly seeped into the operations of the state and the passing of new laws. Emperors began outlawing the festivities on Sundays and holidays, and then eventually Christian emperors ended the gladiator games forever.

Like the gladiator games, the culture of Roman theater offended Christian morals. Christianity didn't oppose theater per se but strongly objected to the depravity reflected in the art's culture. Roman theater exhibited bawdy and brutal performances that exploited women and children. Audiences at times demanded that women appear naked, and some emperors required actors to engage in sexual acts on stage.

Christian leaders moved more carefully in their stand against the theater than they did in their stand against the games. Many new converts lived among the working class, which included actors. Taking an aggressive stand against the theater would alienate many members of the church.

Rather than taking a strong, universal stand against the theater, church leaders banned priests from attending the theater. The state later banned productions on Sundays and holidays. Over time, the Roman government passed ordinances to protect the church's interest and forbade the abuse of boys and women.

Jesus' Impact: Sanctity of Life

"I have come that they may have life, and have it to the full." (John 10:10)

While these measures began to affect the Roman theater, attacks by the Visigoths and other groups around AD 410 eventually made the theater both irrelevant and unaffordable.

AUGUSTINE AND THE CITY OF GOD

Throughout Israel's history, the northern and southern kingdoms focused on their position in this world. And throughout their history, God urged the Israelites through the prophets to focus on their hearts. Jesus echoed this teaching, calling the people who followed Him to seek God's kingdom rather than worry about earthly status or position.

As the Christian church assumed power, it began to focus more on the kingdom of this earth and earthly riches. As Christians rose to the highest positions in government—even becoming emperors—they began to confuse God's blessing with the power and wealth of the empire.

When the Visigoths attacked Rome, Christians grew disillusioned. How could God allow the attack of Rome? In contrast, those who held to pagan beliefs blamed Christians: They believed the pagan gods allowed this attack as judgment on an empire that abandoned the pantheon of Roman gods in favor of Christ.

Augustine (AD 354–430) wrote a book, *The City of God*, to defend Christians and Christianity

The Sack of Rome, Joseph Noël Sylvestre (1847–1926)

Painting of St. Augustine from Augustinus Church, Vienna (c. 1875)

in Rome, as well as to refocus Christians' hearts on their real home. Today's church holds Augustine as the greatest Christian theologian since the apostle Paul. Born in a small town in North Africa, Augustine grew up learning from tutors who focused on many different philosophies as well as on rhetoric. After moving to Milan in northern Italy (in AD 383), he concentrated his learning on the teachings of Plato.

Augustine converted to Christianity at the age of thirty-one after meeting Ambrose, the bishop of Milan. Ambrose likely influenced the conversion of the young Augustine and his subsequent training in the scriptures. After his conversion, Augustine returned home, settling in Hippo (the modern-day town of Annaba, Algeria). While living in Hippo, he served as presbyter in the church and ultimately as bishop. Augustine devoted his life to the study of God's Word, giving up his worldly possessions for a life of austerity. He died at the age of seventy-five.

Best known for his writing, Augustine composed many important books and essays that the church accepted as church doctrine in many cases. His works include titles such as *Confessions*, *City of God*, and *On the Trinity*.

Outspoken in his opposition to contemporary heresies and their teachers, Augustine specifically battled the Pelagians, a group who believed that God gave humanity a second chance after the fall. According to their teachings, someone who lived a good and virtuous life could earn a place in heaven. Augustine fought this teaching, stating that God's grace alone can save humanity. Going further into this theme, he explicitly stated that salvation demonstrated God's mercy, while damnation demonstrated God's judgment.

The church embraced and taught Augustine's writings that covered such diverse areas as the sanctity of human life, sexual morality, health care, justice, slavery, and church government. Today's church still feels the influence of his writings.

IMPACT ON SOCIETY

In order to emphasize our need for salvation, Jesus challenged His followers to "be perfect, therefore, as [their] heavenly Father is perfect" (Matthew 5:48). As the centuries drew on, some began to emphasize this challenge by turning away from earthly pleasures and finding ways to devote themselves to spiritual living. This emphasis caused the rise of monasticism.

Early monks lived as hermits. Living in solitude allowed them to focus on the self-discipline they believed would lead to a sanctified life. They established themselves in remote areas of the desert for the purpose of solitary prayer and study. Over time monks became less reclusive and began to teach others and live among others. By the fifth century, most monks lived in cenobitic communes (communal living).

Jesus' Impact: Holy Living

"Be perfect, therefore, as your heavenly Father is perfect." (Matthew 5:48)

While individual monasteries varied, monks in each studied scriptures and early church writings. Monks increased in biblical scholarship in an illiterate society. They followed the scriptural admonition to "study to shew thyself approved unto God" (2 Timothy 2:15 KJV). The knowledge that these monks gained gave them considerable influence in the area of education—especially since they were usually the only educated people within their surrounding communities.

In AD 370, Basil the Great (AD 330–379) rose to the rank of bishop of Caesarea. He believed that the monasteries should remain as part of the church and helped bring them under the authority of bishops. He also believed that the monks could positively impact the community by serving the people. This effort was consistent with

Statue detail of a priest or monk with a cross

Jesus' teaching when He reminded His followers not to hide their light (Luke 11:33) but to intentionally love God and love others. The monasteries under Basil reached out to Caesarea (in Palestine), helping the sick and providing education to the people.

As the monks began working within the communities, they had both positive and adverse effects. While they defended Christianity and helped refine orthodox doctrine, some were led by their zeal to loot and destroy pagan temples.

IMPACT ON LEARNING

The monk Cassiodorus (c. AD 490–583) sought to advance the education of his brethren and founded a monastery near the Ionian Sea that focused on education. He expected monks living in his monastery to complete the readings of his "Institutions," a collection of works that included classical

Christian texts as well as excerpts of medieval liberal arts, giving his monks a wide spiritual and secular education.

The monastery of Cassiodorus helped preserve many Greco-Roman books and influenced other monasteries to do the same. Their reach went so far that one church scholar credits the faraway Celtic monasteries with saving much of Latin literature when Rome fell (see *How the Irish Saved Civilization* by Cahill).

A generation later, Saint Benedict founded the first Benedictine monastery in Monte Cassino, Italy (c. AD 529). The focus of his monasteries also followed the trend toward scholarship and education. The monks in this order worked to preserve the Christian faith and built significant libraries that housed classic works of literature.

As centers of learning, monasteries served as the first Christian universities. The ruling and wealthy class sought out monks for their knowledge and gave them influence with the rich and powerful. Monks functioned as counselors and advisers from this time period and throughout the Middle Ages.

IMPACT ON LEGAL CODES

The teaching and moral code of Jesus has had an effect on every legal code in Western civilization. By the early fifth century, a Christianized Rome sought to review and consolidate its complex law code. The Romans especially desired to catalog laws created under Christian influence. Theodosius II made the

first attempt at this between circa AD 429 and 438, creating the *Codex Theodosianus*. This codex listed only those laws enacted by the state since Rome had yielded to a Christian worldview. That made it clear that any laws from before that time were immaterial. Nevertheless, pagan influences remained in Roman law, along with laws clearly influenced by the Christian faith and beliefs.

Although the codex helped, Roman law remained complex and difficult to enforce. To help solidify and maintain the law, Emperor Justinian established a committee of legal scholars to create a code of civil law, known as the Justinian Code. This code included Roman influence and also laws inspired by

Lady Justice, Frankfurt, Germany

the teachings of Christ. Working from circa AD 529 to 534, the scholars produced four volumes:

1. The *Codex* contained the actual laws of the empire.
2. The *Digest* was compiled from writings by classic jurists regarding the law.
3. The *Institutes* summarized the law and became a legal textbook.
4. The *Novels* contained laws passed after AD 534.

Essentially all legal codes in the Western world derive their roots from this document. Over a thousand years later, the English common law—which was influenced by Justinian's code—became the foundation of the US legal code.

QUESTIONS

1. In what ways did Constantine's actions change the church?

2. How would you describe the central issues of the Nicene Council?

3. How would you describe the relationship between the church and government after Constantine?

4. In what ways did Jesus change the calendar?

5. Why did Christians oppose certain forms of entertainment?

6. What early impact did monasticism have on society?

Chapter 3

THE IMPACT OF JESUS ON THE EARLY MIDDLE AGES
(Approximately AD 500–1100)

Jesus reserved His harshest condemnations for the religious elite who sought power over genuine faith. He confronted the Pharisees by calling them "snakes" (Matthew 23:33) because of the slippery way they slid into positions of power in people's lives. He also called them "whitewashed tombs" (Matthew 23:27). While they appeared pristine and sparkling on the outside, they were filled with death and decay on the inside. If there was a message the leaders of the Middle Ages church needed to hear, it was this one.

During the time of the Middle Ages, leaders wore the trappings of Christianity in order to maintain power over others. Although this time period included many positive advancements introduced by the church, its leaders corrupted themselves with power.

Ancient sarcophagus (a "whitewashed tomb") discovered in Jerusalem

By the time of the Middle Ages, the Catholic Church and the Roman Empire were linked inseparably. Christian teaching and doctrine permeated every area of life. Monasteries surfaced as the seat of learning, as monks studied both spiritual and secular subjects and used their knowledge to help the communities around them.

**Jesus' Impact:
Righteousness of God**

"Woe to you, teachers of the law and Pharisees, you hypocrites! You are like whitewashed tombs, which look beautiful on the outside but on the inside are full of the bones of the dead and everything unclean." (Matthew 23:27)

Saint Benedict Monastery near Subiaco, Lazio, Italy

The Roman government and the church observed a clear line between them. However, the leaders of the church maintained a strong influence on government leaders and their policies, and vice versa. While this often brought good changes, Christian leaders demonstrated venal and carnal behavior. Nevertheless, the influence of the church—and ultimately the teachings of Jesus—pushed culture forward.

MONASTERIES, LITERACY, AND ACADEMICS

Monasteries sprang up across the Roman Empire, offering a chance for spiritual growth and education to those called to a life of serving Jesus. As time went on, the difference between the Eastern and Western monasteries grew, becoming more pronounced. While both held to many of the same practices, their lifestyles sprang from differing motivation.

Western monasticism emphasized community, while their Eastern counterparts focused on solitude. This core value drove how each group punished their own bodies. While both groups punished the flesh as a means of training, Western monasticism viewed discipline as a way to train the body, mind, and soul, so that the individual would be ready to fulfill his work in the world. In contrast, those within Eastern monasticism disciplined themselves for the primary purpose of renunciation of sin. Both approaches emphasized different teachings of Jesus:

- West (training the body): "Whoever wants to be my disciple must deny themselves and take up their cross and follow me." (Mark 8:34)
- East (focusing on piety): "Pray that you will not fall into temptation." (Luke 22:40)

Saint Benedict handing down his rule to monks of his order. Monastery of St. Giles, Nimes, France (1129)

We see this basic difference between community and solitude reflecting in the monks' relationship with the church. Western monasteries worked as the strong right arm of the popes, bishops, and other ecclesiastical leaders. Eastern monasteries, however, tended to be at odds with the church leaders, often speaking out against sin and corruption.

Saint Benedict of Nursia (c. AD 480–543/547) influenced culture more than any other church leader in this time period. He founded many monasteries himself, the most widely known being the Monte Cassino in central Italy. Possibly while staying at the Monastery of Saint Gilles in Nimes, France, he wrote his famous *Rule of Benedict*—comprised of seventy-three chapters that laid out the proper relationship between a monk and his abbot, community, and daily life.

Benedict's rules emphasized that a monk should remain in the same monastery throughout the entire time of his service; he should not travel from one monastery to another without accountability to authority. An exception would only be made if he were ordered to move. While monasteries received monks who had withdrawn from the community and returned, these monks could only be received back twice. On each occurrence, they would be reinstated at the lowest rank, as a test of their humility.

These monks valued humility and obedience, following the example of Jesus. Leaving a monastery could be seen as an act of rebellion against the authority of the abbot and others placed in positions of authority over the monk. If unwilling to submit to those placed in visible authority over them, how could a monk ever be expected to submit fully to an invisible God?

Monks treasured their studies. Centuries earlier, Paul wrote to Timothy, "Study to shew thyself approved" (2 Timothy 2:15 KJV). This call to discipline continued Jesus' urge to "love the Lord your God with all your heart and with all your soul and with all your strength and with all your *mind*" (Luke 10:27, emphasis added). In an effort to fulfill this charge, monks carefully examined

The founders of Benedictine monasticism, Saint Benedict and Saint Scholastica, depicted on a stained-glass window

both Christian and secular texts, becoming the best-educated men in the empire. The libraries of the various monasteries emerged as the depositories of knowledge in the Roman Empire, with the monks both studying and preserving that knowledge.

Benedict himself constantly searched out new books to read and study. He personally built many of the libraries in the monasteries he established.

In a world without printing presses, monks copied old texts to preserve teaching and to repair fragile and damaged copies. This exhausting task, often done in harsh working conditions, lasted as a great contribution of monasteries. Their work preserved ancient Latin literature, saving these texts from mold, mildew, rats, and decay.

Artist representation of Saint Bede, original artist unknown

Authors L. D. Reynolds and N. G. Wilson described the importance of transcribing these volumes: "At one swoop a number of texts were recovered which might otherwise have been lost forever; to this one monastery in this one period we owe the preservation of the later *Annals* and *Histories* of Tacitus (Plate XIV), the *Golden Ass* of Apuleius, the *Dialogues* of Seneca, Varro's *De lingua latina*,

Frontinus' *De aquis*, and thirty-odd lines of Juvenal's sixth satire that are not to be found in any other manuscript."[1]

Many monks joined Benedict in scholarly studies, but their names have been forgotten by history. One English monk, Venerable Bede (AD 672/673–735) studied so fervently that he acquired the name "The Father of English History." Had it not been for his studying, teaching, and writing, a large part of English history would probably have been lost.

The Preservation of Classic Literature

Had it not been for the monks, centuries of classic literature would have been lost. After the fall of Rome, Irish monks passed throughout the Roman Empire and collected all the written works that they could. They preserved the priceless literature in the monasteries of their island, saving it from being thrown on the trash heap of history.

Monks often sought to share their knowledge and opened schools for the education of children. While open to all, children of nobility attended most frequently, as lower-class children worked alongside their parents and could not afford leisure time for studies.

Although the schools met in the monasteries, they taught much more than the Bible. The monks who taught sought to prepare children of noble birth to fulfill their responsibilities as adults. These schools foreshadowed universities that existed later. These monks valued all disciplines and exposed their students to history, science, and philosophy.

Although popes and bishops supported the monasteries, these monastic communities could not afford a life of mere leisure and study. Monks worked in other ventures, including agriculture, to provide for themselves.

Monks in the early Middle Ages developed great building skills; they built monasteries that have stood over a thousand years and helped to develop their nearby towns and communities. While some monks developed skills and crafts, they urged one another not to take pride in their work but to work as an act of service and worship to God (Romans 12:1–2). With this spirit, their work was given to the advancement of the community rather than seen as personal advancement.

Monks applied the early church teaching of 2 Thessalonians 3:10 ("The one who is unwilling to work shall not eat") and often grew the food that they ate. They developed and improved water systems for both drinking and irrigation, and also developed many new agricultural techniques. This drive for agriculture advancement grew from their great need. Because monks often built monasteries on land deeded to them, they found their communities built in wild and inaccessible places. The residents of monasteries learned to develop creative farming techniques in order to simply feed themselves.

Since monks aspired to humility, following the teachings of Jesus, they embraced lowly work that others avoided. Known for their extremely good work ethic, monks made land usable for agriculture by building dikes, draining swampland, and clearing vast quantities of land. They conserved God's earth by planting carefully selected trees in the areas that they cleared.

Monks and Agriculture

Monks also farmed in ways that conserved water, such as using retaining walls and implementing terraced farming.

Monks often supplied water to communities during times of drought. They typically stored water, which enabled them to practically apply Christ's teaching to share water with the thirsty (Matthew 25:35–40).

As monks farmed, their studious habits led them to study the results of their work. They discovered that certain types of crops grew best in certain types of soil and within certain types of environments.

Communication between monks and other monasteries allowed for the sharing of agricultural advances. Monks also taught what they learned to

Miniature painting of medieval farmers from *The Very Rich Hours of the Duke of Berry*, Barthélemy d'Eyck (1444–1469)

people in their community, introducing new methods to help improve farming. Some of the agricultural methods that have been attributed to monks include cattle breeding, beer and wine making, bee raising, fish farming, cheese making, and fruit and corn growing. Monks also discovered the benefits of some phosphate fertilizers; they spread the slag from their forges (which was high in phosphates) on their fields.

Beyond the fields, monks developed waterpower that transformed industries. They harnessed the power of water for milling grain, sieving flour, fulling (or cleaning) cloth, and tanning hides.

Old water mill on the Hain River, Belgium

The monks viewed manual work, especially difficult and unattractive labor, as a means of disciplining the flesh and receiving God's grace. They embraced farming in a society where farming had begun to lose its social appeal. Their example and work ethic gave a new dignity to farming and to the selflessness of community living in the body of Christ.

Because monks often produced more than they needed from their farming efforts, the local abbot traded their excess with the community for things that the monastery needed. This added to the self-sufficiency of the monastery. Some monasteries even amassed riches, to the point where they hired others to do their work, allowing monks more time to study.

**Jesus' Impact:
Caring for the Poor**

"For I was hungry and you gave me something to eat, I was thirsty and you gave me something to drink, I was a stranger and you invited me in." (Matthew 25:35)

In an effort to love and serve God with all their minds, monks studied and gained all kinds of knowledge wherever it could be found. While Christian works and philosophy dominated their studies, they also included secular works. A monk named Cassiodorus Senator (c. AD 490–585) studied pagan literature extensively. In his monastery, which he founded in Vivarium, Italy, he required the study of these texts by those in his fellowship.

After the Roman Empire divided in AD 395, the western part further divided into separate fiefdoms. These fiefdoms stood largely cut off from the rest of the world by the Eastern Roman Empire. Nevertheless, the vast majority of the people maintained their Christian roots and their connection to the Roman Catholic Church.

Philosophy in Western Europe developed independently from the rest of the world. Philosophical discoveries fed the hunger for additional discoveries. Jesus' teaching (and the rest of the Bible) strongly influenced the study of every discipline—including philosophy, science, and history—which often meant that Christian doctrine was the foundation or premise of each discipline.

Boethius teaching his students, *Consolation of Philosophy* (1935)

Italian manuscript of the *Consolation of Philosophy* (1935) showing a hand-printed miniature of Boethius teaching in prison

From this viewpoint, the Middle Ages uplifted both Christianity and learning. Science served to support the Bible, rather than to try and disprove it. Philosophical discovery aimed to support scripture in some way and was often used to support the veracity of the Bible as God's own Word to humankind. The Bible served as the starting point of all study, with serious scholars expanding their studies and experimentation outward from there.

One of the greatest Christian philosophers in Europe during the Middle Ages was Boethius (c. AD 480–524). Born to a prominent Roman family, he was orphaned at a young age and raised by a nobleman. He gained wide respect among the nobility for his scholarship and intelligence. His reputation led to his service to Theodoric the Great (AD 454–526), the Germanic king of the Ostrogoths in the Eastern Roman Empire.

Boethius held many important positions under Theodoric. As he worked for Theodoric, Boethius worked to revitalize the relationship between the church in Rome and the church in Constantinople. The bishops of these two cities verbally sparred with one another. Unfortunately, some contemporary leaders viewed Boethius's work as an attempt to reunify the Roman Empire instead of the church. Due to speculation, Boethius was imprisoned and eventually executed as a traitor.

Boethius

While awaiting execution, Boethius wrote his greatest work, *De Consolatione Philosophiae* (*The Consolation of Philosophy*). In this volume, he waxed philosophically about the flightiness of the favor of princes and the lack of consistency in the devotion of friends.

Until the twelfth century, Boethius's work was the primary source of information on Aristotle. His works also had a strong influence on later philosophers. In addition to his own work, Boethius translated the work of many classic philosophers.

Christianity and art have a long, tumultuous relationship. Church leaders in the early Middle Ages debated over whether there was any place for fine art within the church. Sharp division existed, with very little room for opinions that offered middle ground.

The debate understandably stems from the Ten Commandments, where God states, "You shall not make for yourself an image in the form of anything in heaven above or on the earth beneath or in the waters below. You shall not bow down to them or worship them" (Exodus 20:4–5). Some viewed the first part of that passage

Art and Christianity

In many ways, art was a necessity to the advancement of Christianity. However, the line between viewing and worshipping art blurred throughout church history. Jesus affirmed the second commandment when He was tempted by Satan in the wilderness: "Worship the Lord your God, and serve him only" (Matthew 4:10). Protestants—who adhered to Jesus' command to worship God alone—denounced the Roman Catholic use of statues of the saints in the church as a form of worship because the faithful would pray to those statues.

Statue of the Virgin Mary carrying the infant Jesus

Art from the catacombs of Rome. Date and artist unknown.

of scripture as denying Christians the right to make any images whatsoever. Others insisted that art violated God's command only if created for the purpose of worshipping it. Those holding the latter view pointed to the beautiful images and designs that adorned the ancient tabernacle and temples of the Hebrew people.

In the Middle Ages, hand-copied Bibles were scarce and printed copies did not yet exist. Even if they had been available, few people could read them, as the vast majority of the people remained illiterate. Christian art taught the Bible to common people. Much like a picture Bible might give today's child an introduction to the Bible, this art introduced illiterate church attendees to important Bible stories and doctrines.

Before the marriage of the church and the Roman Empire, society offered few outlets for Christian artists. Drawings on the ancient Christian catacomb walls show all that remains of this early form of Christian art.

Once the church was officially recognized by Rome, Christian art flourished. The state permitted such art and the church commissioned it, which allowed artists to thrive and the art industry to grow. Other than portraits of royalty and wealthy individuals, almost all the surviving Middle Age art depicts Christian themes or biblical events and stories rendered in paintings, sculptures, stained glass, and mosaics.

An old engraving showing monks at work, *History of the Church* (c. 1880)

Artists tried to portray the paradox between the transcendent and the immanent, the spiritual and the material. Many artists also applied their skills to creating utilitarian objects in the church—such as the crucifixes, chalices, and candle stands used especially for the celebration of the Mass. Many of these intricate objects were painstakingly carved.

As monks copied the Bible, they illuminated the pages, which consisted of elegantly decorating the pages with ink and precious metals. This illustration and design work ranged from creating highly decorated first letters for chapters to adding floral borders, sidebars, margins, headers, and footers. In some cases, the illumination allowed for little text on the page. At times, artists created illumination using gold or silver leaf or paint. Originally, it was viewed that only the Bible merited the illumination of text; however, over time, scribes illuminated other important texts as well.

While illuminated manuscripts could take on any form, most often scribes assembled them in a codex, which helped to preserve their art for a thousand years. (Codices are books that are bound on one edge and made up of sheets of paper, vellum,

Jesus' Impact: Idol Worship

"It is written: 'Worship the Lord your God, and serve him only.' " (Matthew 4:10; Luke 4:8)

The Baptism of Christ (c. 1475), Andrea del Verrocchio (c. 1436–1488) and Leonardo da Vinci (1452–1519)

or papyrus. Their covers protect the pages from damage. Often scribes used leather to cover these books, which is the reason many still exist today.)

In the eastern part of the empire, the church (which ultimately formed the Eastern Orthodox Church) turned to the painting of icons, which often depicted Jesus, Mary, angels, or various saints. These panels taught biblical stories and preserved the testimonies of historical church leaders who had died. The Eastern Orthodox Church venerated and honored icons, seemingly in direct violation of Jesus' teaching against idolatry. Strong conflicting views about the appropriate use of icons created points of contention between the Eastern and Western churches.

Arab power increased in the Byzantine Empire in the seventh century. This brought with it a revival in Islamic art, which was rejected by the church. Ultimately, the church of the East banned artwork that represented any religious image. In response, many Christian artists moved to Rome, where they could openly create their art. Others abandoned the church and moved to Eastern Arab lands.

DIVINE RIGHTS AND ALLIANCES

When the Western Roman Empire finally fell in AD 476, the church offered a stabilizing influence in society, helping to maintain civilized order. This continued to increase the influence of the Western church so that it often stood as the de facto—albeit temporary—government. The church had trouble relinquishing authority once local governments rose up. The release

Fresco of the coronation of Charlemagne (c. sixteenth century), at the Vatican Museum

was often conditional, with the church maintaining some control over the ruling feudal lords.

Western Europe moved toward feudal empires, with strong noblemen taking what lands they could. Often, to gain legitimacy, they sought the approval of the church. As a result, local bishops customarily crowned kings. The Franks (tribes that lived in the area of modern-day France and Germany) supported this practice, affirming that the church had the authority to choose whom to crown as king.

Charlemagne, king of the Franks during the Holy Roman Empire (c. late 700s)

The concept of a divine right of kings grew from this practice. It was understood that the kings ruled because God chose them to rule. With this understanding, kings were expected to lean heavily on power and reputation and receive the submission and respect of their subjects (Hebrews 13:17).

Unfortunately, this shared power between the church and state ultimately led to darkness. Rulers like Charlemagne (c. AD 747–814) and Otto I (AD 912–973) invaded countries and regions on behalf of the pope. In turn, the pope rewarded them with the crown of the conquered territories.

Because of the strong alliances that existed between many rulers and the church, the church gave rulers perceived legitimacy and the rulers forced conquered people to convert to Christianity—with the church's blessing, of course. One of these symbiotic alliances grew between the Franks and the papacy in Rome—a relationship that affected politics and religion for centuries. The Franks protected the church; the church protected the ruler's power. It was a seemingly win-win situation.

One of the practical outcomes was the unhealthy way the church helped the secular rulers to control the people. Rebellion against the crown would be seen as rebellion against God's anointed representative. To resist the crown was to resist God. The threat of excommunication, with the associated risk of the church's threat to doom someone to the fires of hell, was a very strong inducement toward obedience. Few would willingly rebel against the authority of the crown.

Rulers rose and fell with the constant tides of war. The lords would go to battle against one another, losing or gaining lands and honor. Often, victorious lords paid their armies by giving them lands that had been conquered. Since those who had received the lands no longer needed the lords to protect them, they would sometimes attack the very same lords from whom they had received the land. This created a never-ending cycle of war, with the church caught right in the middle.

While the church and the rulers worked together, they did so with great difficulty. Although the rulers avowed to be Christians, the fervor of their apparent faith was affected by a lust for power. This left them, at

The Church and Nobility

The church helped unify small fiefdoms into larger countries. The rulers of those countries depended on the church to affirm their right to rule and help them control the people. Bishops counseled the nobility, helping to shape the course taken by those rulers.

Jesus receiving the Magdeburg Cathedral from Emperor Otto I (c. 962–968)

times, at odds with the church hierarchy. Church leaders threatened excommunication and used manipulation to control the leaders, just as they did with the common people.

In this turbulent atmosphere, a constant struggle for supremacy lasted between the secular rulers and religious leaders. While the rulers had the strength of arms to back them, the church threatened eternal destinies. In the end, the perceived ability to wield eternal outcomes provided a

Jesus' Impact:
Authority of God

"Are you the king of the Jews?" asked Pilate. "You have said so," Jesus replied. (Mark 15:2; Luke 23:3)

trump card of power for the church. Sadly, church leaders grew addicted to power, as did the secular rulers. Power, though often disguised by a religious tapestry of words, served as the end in itself.

In the minds of the church leaders, their power play was seemingly justified by the teaching of Jesus, who spoke of a kingdom at odds with this world (John 15:18–19; 18:36). But Jesus sought to influence the hearts of people, not to control them. It was a corrupted church—not Christ's teaching—that led to earthly power struggles.

THE GROUNDWORK FOR SCHISM

When Constantine brought the bishops together for the first ecumenical council in Nicaea in AD 325, he recognized the need for a more structured church government. Independent bishops over individual cities led to social and theological disunity. To solve this, five patriarchs were given charge over regions to govern the bishops and churches within those regions. The council selected bishops as patriarchs over the cities of Rome, Alexandria, Antioch, and Jerusalem, followed by Constantinople in AD 330. The bishop of Rome assumed the title *pope* to separate himself from the other patriarchs and declared his authority over the other patriarchs.

The patriarchs immediately struggled for power. All agreed that the pope of Rome deserved higher honor than the other patriarchs, but not necessarily greater authority. Ultimately, the struggle crystallized between the pope of Rome and the patriarch of Constantinople. One wielded power in the Western church and the other resided close to the emperor in the capital of the Byzantine Empire.

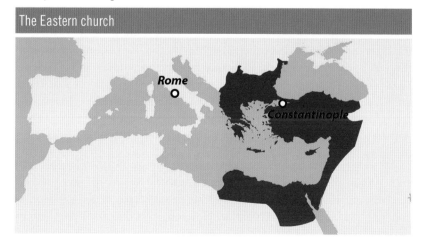

The Eastern church

Rome

Constantinople

Jesus had prayed that His disciples would be one, as He and the Father were one (John 17:11). Sadly, pride got in the way of attaining this type of unity within the leadership of the church, with the pope of Rome and the bishop of Constantinople both claiming supremacy. Their pride and lust for power blinded them to the spirit behind Jesus' teaching and prayers for unity in John 17.

The main points of disagreement between the Eastern and Western churches were exacerbated when the Roman Empire divided. Some of these disagreements centered on theological terms, but many focused on cultural differences.

DISAGREEMENTS BETWEEN THE EAST AND WEST

Many years after the Nicene Creed was written (AD 325), the bishop of Rome prevailed in adding the *filioque* clause to the Nicene Creed (AD 589). This clause, in the second part of the creed, defines that the Holy Spirit came from the Father *and the Son*. (Originally, the Creed stated that the Holy Spirit came only from the Father.) The Eastern church disagreed with this addition and never accepted it.

The Western church disagreed with the Eastern use of icons in their churches and worship, calling it a form of idolatry. At the same time, Islamic scholars pointed to the use of images in the Western church as being a form of polytheistic idolatry.

Islam posed a number of challenges to the church in the East. As Islam rose, the Byzantine Empire desperately fought with the Persian Empire between the sixth and ninth centuries. To finance the long war, the Byzantine government taxed their provinces heavily and alienated the people. In contrast, Islam offered people an opportunity for conquest, position, and riches. Since many of the residents of the Eastern Byzantine Empire were of Semitic origins, they found the lure of their Eastern, Persian neighbors appealing, and a number of them defected.

In addition, the Eastern and Western churches related to governmental authority differently. In the East, the church submitted to the emperor, as had been established by Constantine. However, with the fall of the Western

Roman Empire, the Western church was independent. Generally, Western secular rulers submitted to the church.

Cultural differences drove a wedge between the East and West as well. Islam influenced the East; barbarians influenced the West. As years went on, the single culture once propagated by the unified empire splintered and gave way to different languages and customs.

Pope Leo III (c. AD 750–816) crowned Charlemagne emperor on December 25, 800. This coronation exacerbated tensions between the East and West. Charlemagne (the king of the Franks) could lay claim to the Eastern Byzantine Empire. However, that empire refused to acknowledge Charlemagne's coronation and believed he had overstepped his authority.

Ancient Orthodox icon

The rise of Islam greatly affected the spread of Christianity. Islamic history maintains that Mohammed (c. AD 570–632) received a vision while living in Mecca. This vision led to the birth of Islam. Although he gathered a small following, the people of Mecca ultimately rejected his teaching and banished him. Mohammed fled to Medina, where he and his followers conquered the city. By the time he died two years later, he had converted most of the Arabian Peninsula to Islam.

The Saracen (Muslim) Army outside Paris, Julius Schnorr von Carolsfeld (1794–1872)

Mohammed and his followers continued evangelizing by the sword and threat of violence. By the time Mohammed died in AD 632, Muslims controlled the bulk of the Arabian Peninsula. Upon Mohammed's death, the leadership of Islam passed to the caliphs, who served as religious and civil leaders.

The first caliph, Abu Bakr (c. AD 573–634), consolidated the territory under Muslim control and then began a series of conquests. Although he ruled for only two years before his death, he made major strides in spreading Islam to the East and West. The caliphs defeated the Sasanian Empire in 640, which held the remains of the old Persian Empire. This greatly expanded the territory under Muslim control. The conquest of Egypt followed shortly afterward, beginning in 642.

After these conquests, the caliphs launched an attack against the Byzantine Empire. Their expansion northward was both military and social. The racial and cultural similarities between the Arabs and the residents of the Byzantine Empire appealed to many people who were under the control of the Byzantines and disillusioned with their government's heavy taxes to finance long-standing wars with Persia.

Muslims Conquer Persia

The war that the Byzantines had been fighting against the Persians contributed to the rise of Islam. Years of fighting and weakening the Persians may have made it easier for the Muslims to conquer Persia.

Before the rise of Islam, the power and influence of the Eastern and Western churches may have been fairly equal. During this time, however, the East boasted more churches and offered greater riches

Battle between the Byzantines and the Persians, Piero della Francesca (1415–1492)

than those in the West. Three of the five church patriarchs resided in the East. However, they could not stem the tide of Islam, which was borne along by the waves of war.

Many of the Eastern centers of Christianity fell to Muslim rule, including Jerusalem, Antioch, Damascus, Alexandria, and Carthage. These cities contained five of the largest churches in Christian lands. In Carthage and the surrounding areas, Christianity completely disappeared. In many of the other areas, it was lightly tolerated. The Christian church ceased to grow in Muslim-controlled lands and barely survived in those places.

As Islam expanded, its leaders gained loyalty with their new subjects by investing in the territories they conquered. Typically, Muslims left the conquered lands largely undisturbed but pressured the people to convert to Islam.

At the same time that Islam spread to the east and north, it also spread westward from Egypt as the Muslims conquered North Africa. By the year AD 711, they invaded Spain from the south. They conquered it in 718.

Spain prospered under Muslim rule. The Muslims permitted Spanish Christians and Jews to practice their religions but taxed them heavily. Many converted to Islam to avoid the financial burden, and all people lived under sharia law.

Constantinople managed to hold firm and stopped the spread of Islam farther into Europe from the East. Although Muslims raided the region and brought the city under siege two times, they never defeated the Byzantines.

On the western side of Europe, Charles Martel, the duke and prince of the Franks (c. AD 688–741), stopped an Islamic advance in Spain in AD 721. Martel held the title of mayor of the palace of Austrasia (a title he had inherited from his father). His position gave him exceptional power over the Frankish throne, with the local king serving more as a figurehead. Martel's life as a fighter, battling for power and position, prepared him for a fresh attack by the Muslim Spanish Moors. He stopped them cold when they came across the Pyrenees Mountains, defeating them again

Charlemagne's Coronation

Pope Leo's coronation of Charlemagne may have been more of a political maneuver rather than a reward for services rendered. Charlemagne's father, Pippin, had given the pope the lands around Rome. The nature of this gift makes it seem that Pippin, as king, had possessed greater authority than the pope. By being the one to crown Charlemagne, the pope would have established his own authority over the emperor.

and killing the Islamic governor of the city of Cordoba in Spain, Abd-ar-Rahman, in 732. This earned him the nickname "The Hammer."

Charlemagne receives the submission of Widukind, the Germanic leader of the Saxons, in Paderborn, Germany

This major defeat for the Muslims stopped the expansion of their dominion. Along with the Byzantines' efforts against the Muslims in the East, Martel's victory secured Europe and prevented it from becoming a part of the Islamic world.

Upon the death of King Theuderic IV (c. AD 712–737), Martel assumed the leadership of the Franks, although he wasn't legally king. Even without a crown, he acted as king and divided the kingdom between his two sons upon his death.

Before dying, Martel pushed the Muslims back into Spanish territory, beginning the Reconquista. His son Pippin the Younger (c. AD 714–768) and his grandson Charlemagne continued his work. Although Charlemagne fought all his life, he focused his efforts on battles to spread Christianity northward and eastward, rather than fighting against the Muslims. Charlemagne fought the Saxons and traveled as far as the Slavic nations, spreading Christianity. His work to spread the influence of the church led Pope Leo III to crown him emperor of Rome in AD 800—the first emperor to rule over Rome in over three hundred years.

EFFECTS ON HANDWRITING

The Carolingian Renaissance began under the reign of Pippen the Younger (AD 751) and came to full bloom under Charlemagne (AD 800). During this time, literature, the arts and architecture, and reforms in the church's liturgy flourished.

This renaissance helped preserve scripture, as well as other ancient texts from early Roman times. Up until this time, the monks who transcribed the texts used the Merovingian script, which was characterized by a lack of punctuation, spacing, and capital letters.

Because the Merovingian script proved difficult to read and copy, even careful scribes inadvertently introduced errors with each copy. These errors could make it impossible to

Charlemagne and Literacy

Although Charlemagne recognized the value of the written word and the importance of having a uniform script, he was never fully literate himself.

understand the original intent of the written work. While almost 90 percent of surviving ancient Roman texts contain Carolingian manuscript, the original scribes likely used Merovingian script.

Statue of Pippin the Younger, who began the process of improving handwriting. This led to the establishment of the writing style known as Carolingian minuscule.

When Pippin the Younger took over the throne, he set a goal of raising the intellectual level of the clergy first and then, through them, that of his subjects. This desire continued when Charlemagne later introduced the Carolingian minuscule, invented by Maurdramnus, the abbot of Corbie. This style emerged as the standard writing style for Latin, as it was much clearer to read and saved space on the page. In need of assistance in educating the masses, Charlemagne brought the English scholar Alcuin of York to his court; together they established a library and taught the Carolingian minuscule.

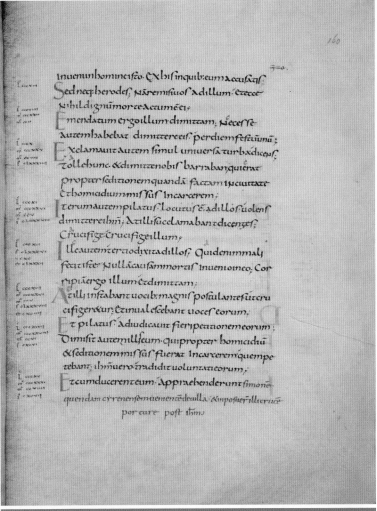

Text of Luke 23:14–26 from a Carolingian Gospel book written in Carolingian minuscule

Jesus' Impact:
Preservation of the Word of God

"If you hold to my teaching, you are really my disciples. Then you will know the truth, and the truth will set you free." (John 8:31–32)

Readers found many differences between the Carolingian minuscule and the Merovingian script. This newer script used clear capital letters, making it obvious where new sentences began. Spaces between words eliminated the misunderstandings created by not knowing where a word ended and a new word began. The characters took on a uniform appearance, with rounded shapes that offered clear, distinguishable traits. All this together contributed to making text much more readable, which made the monks' job of studying and transcribing much easier than ever before.

QUESTIONS

1. What were some of the significant differences in how the Eastern and Western monasteries approached the teachings of Jesus?

2. How did Benedict and other monks preserve and encourage Christian and secular education?

3. How did Jesus' teaching influence monks in their various contributions to society?

4. In what ways did Christian philosophy and teaching change Roman culture in the Middle Ages?

5. How did strong alliances between the church and state negatively affect the spread of Christianity in the Middle Ages?

Chapter 4
THE IMPACT OF JESUS ON THE HIGH MIDDLE AGES
(1000–1500)

When Jesus spoke of seeking "first his kingdom" (Matthew 6:33) and laying aside everything to follow Him, He encouraged His followers to allow their faith to drive every aspect of life. According to Jesus, following Him was more than observing rituals or gathering for weekly services. This fundamental challenge drove the first disciples to build their lives on the foundation of Christ's teaching.

Tribute to the foundation of the church in Obuda, Hungary (1358)

The church's inability to maintain a singular focus on Christ led to some dark moments in the High Middle Ages that showed the weakness of humanity. Yet while there were some glaring failures, there were also many significant advancements based on the teaching of Jesus. During this time we see giant strides in literature, learning, school, science, art, and linguistics—influenced by the church and those who followed Christ.

THE SPLIT BETWEEN ROME AND CONSTANTINOPLE

The differences between the East and West became even more pronounced, ultimately leading to a split between the churches. The Western church, or "Holy Roman Church," consolidated its power, while the less-centralized Eastern church battled influences of Muslim invaders.

Problems between the Eastern church and the Western church began shortly after the first Nicene Council in AD 325. Although Jesus had prayed for the unity of the church (John 17), the human leaders of the church lost that vision. From the time of Constantine, power plays between the original five patriarchs set a divisive tone that strained church unity (see chapter 3). As centuries elapsed, the differences grew into great rifts between the church of the East and the church of the West.

Jesus' Impact: Unity of the Church

"Blessed are the peacemakers, for they will be called children of God." (Matthew 5:9)

Finally, in the year AD 1054, the conflict between the pope of Rome (Pope Leo IX) and the patriarch of Constantinople (Michael Cerularius) led to the severe fracture in the relationship between the churches. The two leaders sent letters accusing the other of false doctrine. Cardinal Humbert of Silva Candida (AD 1000–1061) carried Pope Leo's final letter to Cerularius (AD 1000–1059). Along with the letter, the pope gave Humbert the authority to speak and act on his behalf.

Cerularius refused to grant an audience to the cardinal and left him waiting for months. In response, Humbert placed a decree (known as a papal bull) on the altar in the Hagia Sophia in Constantinople. This decree—that came with the authority of the pope in Rome—excommunicated Michael Cerularius and his supporters from the church. Cerularius responded by denouncing the bull and excommunicating the cardinal and the pope's envoy.[1] This event—and the resulting relationship—became known as the East-West Schism (or the Great Schism).

Painting of Pope Leo IX by an unknown artist from an old commune in Alsace, France (c. nineteenth century)

Although the Great Schism occurred in AD 1054, modern-day church historians see signs of the break beginning as far back as AD 589, when the Third Council of Toledo added the filioque clause to the Nicene Creed. (This wording defined church doctrine by stating that the Holy Spirit proceeds from the Father *and* the Son. The Eastern Orthodox Church refused to embrace the change and maintained that the Holy Spirit came only through the Father.) By the tenth century, the clause had been fully accepted by the churches in the West. However, the Eastern churches refused to accept that provision.

The churches fell prey to cultural and racial differences. The dissimilar cultures of Western European Christians and Eastern Arabic Christians led to dissention.[2] The heritage of each yielded different customs and languages. Differing

The Hagia Sophia at night. Of great significance is the Hagia Sophia's place in the splitting of the Eastern (Orthodox) branch of the church from the Western (Roman) branch.

Division within the Church

The Eastern and Western churches attacked each other's practices. The Western church condemned the Eastern church's use of icons. The Eastern church denounced Rome's custom of fasting on Saturday (in honor of the Jewish Sabbath) and the consecration of unleavened bread for Eucharist. Pope Leo IX (AD 1002–1054) labeled Constantinople as the birthplace of heresy and claimed primacy over all the churches and church leaders.

cultures led to different emphases in the Christian life and distinct liturgies. Rather than pursue unity, the two groups focused on differences and upheld their own practices and beliefs as the only faithful gospel.

Pope Leo IX attempted to gain supremacy in the disputes by claiming that the Roman bishop enjoyed a higher position that had been granted by the Donation of Constantine, a document (which was a forgery) that claimed that Constantine transferred his authority over Rome to the bishop of Rome. The Eastern church never accepted this document's validity and correctly called it fraudulent. Nevertheless, Leo used it as his basis to specific papal rights for the bishop of Rome.

During the papacy of Gregory VII (AD 1073–1085), popes began to push back against nobility, seeking independence from imperial domination. A summary of these defenses are within a document titled *Dictatus Papae*, a collection of precedents regarding the pope's authority.

Pope Gregory VII asserted the following:

- Only the authority of the bishop of Rome (whom Western Christians now simply call "the pope") can be called "universal" or "Catholic."
- As the bishop of Rome, he was the only one with the authority to depose and reinstate bishops.
- Use of the imperial symbol was reserved for him alone.
- All princes should bow and kiss the feet of the pope alone.
- He had power over emperors and could depose them.
- No man had the right to judge him or his actions.
- Only those who agreed with the Roman church could be considered Catholic, adhering to the universal faith of the church.
- He alone had the power to absolve an oath of fealty that a subject had made to a wicked ruler.

Adapted from Medieval Sourcebook: Gregory VII: Dictatus Papae 1090 *by Paul Halsall (http://legacy.fordham.edu/halsall/source/g7-dictpap.asp)*

When the patriarch of Constantinople rejected these rights, he also dismissed the authority of the bishop of Rome as pope over the entire church, upholding the traditional role of the bishop of Rome in relation to the other bishops of the church as the first among equals.

A split was inevitable.

THE EFFECTS OF CHRISTIANS ON THE CRUSADES

The Crusades began as religious wars that inspired Christians to attack Muslim-controlled lands. While some people would like to believe these conflicts started with noble ideals, others point to human lusts for power that inspired atrocities, rape, and pillaging. In reality, the Crusades were probably motivated by both factors.

Whatever the motivation for the Crusades, Jesus Christ would never condone the resulting wars. Jesus never urged the rise of an earthly empire but taught His disciples to focus on a heavenly one. He inspired acts of love and mercy, not violence and slaughter. As much as Jesus condemned the Pharisees of His day for their spiritual power play over their followers, He would have had damning words for large-scale bloodshed disguised in a mantle of holy war. Regardless, the Crusades were sold to the people of Europe as a holy war, and the chief salesperson was the pope of Rome.

Christian rulers traditionally held the lands of the Eastern Empire from AD 300 to 500. However, Islamic armies attacked, conquered, and held much of the territory from approximately AD 600 to 1000. Those who lived in conquered lands often had the choice between converting to Islam, death, or a life

Stained glass image of the First Crusade (eleventh-century) in the Cathedral of Saint Michael and Saint Gudula, Brussels, Belgium

similar to slavery. The Muslim conquerors often forcibly took the daughters of Christian families. Furthermore, they rarely permitted the church buildings or other Christian sites to remain but razed them.

Muslims view Islam as the supreme religion over all other religions and view any Muslim who has renounced their faith as an apostate. The crime for living as an apostate (under extreme interpretations of Islamic sharia law) is death.

The Western church used reports of the Muslims' actions to rally men into the Crusades and to stem the tide of Islamic advances. The Eastern church, struggling against Islamic invaders, implored the Western church for help. Pope Urban II (c.1042–1099) unified the church, rallied soldiers to the cause, and aimed to push back the conquests of Islam. In the Council of Clermont of 1095, Urban II called upon the knights of Christendom to rescue their Eastern brethren and retake Jerusalem.

The Pisa Camposanto (cemetery) in Italy, constructed in 1278 to house the holy dirt brought back from Golgotha during the Crusades

The Crusades combined two equally important themes: (1) holy war and (2) a pilgrimage to a holy place. The Crusaders set their sights on Jerusalem, where Jesus had walked and performed many miracles. Because of the nature of the war, the pope promised that true Christians who died in battle would bypass purgatory and directly enter heaven.

The church waged the First Crusade from AD 1096 to 1099, retaking Jerusalem and restoring Nicaea and Antioch to Christian rule. Seven major Crusades followed during the next two hundred years. The Crusaders established a Christian state in Palestine, with its capital in Jerusalem.

While the public policy of this First Crusade allowed conquered people to keep their lands and practice their own religion, gross exceptions to this standard drove some Crusaders to attack Jewish colonies, pillage their towns, and rape their women.

The Taking of Constantinople (or *The Fourth Crusade*), Palma Le Jeune (1544–1620)

About two hundred years after the First Crusade, members of the Fourth Crusade (c. 1201–1204) let underlying tensions inspire them to savagely attack Constantinople. Their despicable actions forever severed relations between the Eastern and Western churches.

While Crusaders have developed a historical reputation for their merciless behavior, they produced some positive advancements. The Crusaders built hospitals in the Middle East and created several religious, medical orders. Study of secular science advanced, as the ideas of East and West were brought together. At the same time, a resurgence of interest in biblical study arose, focusing on the humanity of Jesus. Trade routes between Europe and the Middle East were opened, giving rise to the wealth of cities like Genoa and Venice.

IMPACT ON ARCHITECTURE

The church commissioned most of the large-scale construction during the High Middle Ages. Their building projects outnumbered the government projects and were much grander. Many majestic cathedrals still stand in Europe as a lasting legacy of their work.

As a unifying element of medieval society, the church aimed to create buildings that would glorify God as well as provide built-in Bible lessons. They intentionally built their churches with high ceilings to make people feel small and insignificant and to convey the grandeur of God. They installed stained-glass windows and artwork that portrayed Bible events and served to educate the congregations. The life and teachings of Jesus, captured in art and architecture, impacted the greatest building projects of this period.

Romanesque Churches

The Romanesque style of architecture, developed during this time, varied from earlier types of construction. Chief among the characteristics of Romanesque architecture were the semicircular arched roofs, replacing the wooden roofs used in earlier design. The sanctuary of the church became longer as well, changing from the shape of a T to that of a cross. Finally, a belfry was used to call people to worship.

These Romanesque churches also added a series of small chapels to the sides of the main sanctuary. The chapels weren't used for formal services but to house religious relics. These special memorials encouraged parishioners to focus on Christ and His work as they came into the cathedral for religious services.

Romanesque-style church, Sant Cristòfol of Beget in the Girona Pyrenees, Spain

As the church moved from the eleventh to the twelfth century, the architecture developed into the Gothic style. While the Gothic style was similar to the Romanesque, the arched roofs became pointed. Flying buttresses allowed walls to soar even higher while making them thinner at the same time. These architectural advances added to the grandeur of the cathedrals with even higher ceilings and roofs. Cathedrals were embellished with elaborate stained-glass windows and frescoed paintings, telling the stories of the Bible in pictorial form.

While the Western church moved into Gothic architecture, the Eastern church developed its style of dome roofs. One early example, the Hagia Sophia (Istanbul, Turkey), became the landmark church in the East and one of the largest churches in the world for nearly one thousand years. The style,

The Gothic-style Milan Cathedral in Lombardy, Italy, took nearly six centuries to complete.

often associated with Muslim mosques, was originated by the Byzantine church and adopted by Muslim invaders.

The prevalent feature of the Eastern church later evolved into the onion dome that Russian Orthodox architecture exhibits today. Brightly colored mosaics and icons adorned the interiors of these structures.

Each cathedral or basilica built was designed to stand grander than the next. The church had no shortage of funds; wealth was transferred to the church as people gave generously in hopes of securing God's favor.

IMPACT ON EDUCATION

The work of formally educating the people, began by the monks in the Early Middle Ages, continued and grew throughout the Middle Ages. By the High Middle Ages, not only were the children of the nobility being educated, but some ordinary children were as well.

Saint Basil's Cathedral on Red Square in Moscow, Russia

Another breakthrough in education during this time was the education of girls and young women. While there was an enormous disparity between the number of boys and girls being educated, Christians began providing a wider education to girls. In their efforts to teach both genders, they followed the example of Jesus, who taught both men and women together.

Illumination from Saint Hildegard of Bingen's major work *Scivias* showing her receiving a vision and then relaying it to her secretary

Although the education of girls remained rare, some women began to rise to prominent positions in the church and politics, due in part to the education they received. One woman of the time, Hildegard of Bingen (1098–1179), founded a monastery for women (or a convent) in the twelfth century and regularly corresponded with church leaders.

Jesus' Impact:
The Truth of God's Word

"Do you bring in a lamp to put it under a bowl or a bed? Instead, don't you put it on its stand? For whatever is hidden is meant to be disclosed, and whatever is concealed is meant to be brought out into the open. If anyone has ears to hear, let them hear." (Mark 4:21–23)

Monasteries—especially those of the Benedictine tradition—continued to exist as the seat of learning in the High Middle Ages. The earliest universities were birthed from these monasteries, the first of them being the University of Bologna in Italy, which began near the end of the eleventh century.

Saint Dominic (1170–1221) founded the Dominican Order with an emphasis on education for monks and also for the community surrounding the monastery. Known as great educators, the monks of the Dominican Order included Albert the Great (c. 1200–1280) and Thomas Aquinas (1225–1274).

Thomas Aquinas believed that Christians should study nature as well as the Bible, and that the study of nature would help students to understand the character of God. Through an attempt to know God better, Aquinas emphasized the study of science and logic, furthering Christian studies and general education.

The University of Bologna in Italy, the oldest university in the Western world

While most universities in the Middle Ages began in monasteries, not all were controlled by the church. Some cities founded universities as well. While they were still considered Christian universities, they were not run by the church and their classes were not taught by monks. The bulk of their teaching may have been in agreement with the teachings of Christ, but they were also heavily influenced by Islamic scholars.

The teaching method of these universities became known as Scholasticism, which placed a strong emphasis

The Teaching Method of Scholasticism

Scholasticism used a formalized method of debate known as disputation, in which a tutor presented the topic in the form of a question. (This technique was used by Socrates and other Greek philosophers.) Students would respond with their reasoning, allowing others to dispute it in formal rounds of discussion. Scholasticism married the best of Islamic scholarship with Christian theology and classic philosophy.

Miniature painting by Laurentius de Voltolina (fourteenth century) showing students at the University of Bologna

on dialectical reasoning, inference, and resolving contradictions.

As universities grew, they began to develop local emphases and individual philosophies. The rise of different intellectual movements grew beyond differing opinions as some began to claim that other schools of thought bred heresy. While perhaps true in some cases, it was not true in others.

Although the universities were the centerpieces of education in the Middle Ages, education grew beyond them. Some commoners sought to learn trades as apprentices. Apprenticeships typically started at twelve years of age and were challenging enough to eliminate the possibility of any other studies. Even tradesmen were expected to have a higher level of understanding and knowledge about their trade, making an apprenticeship an important part of an artisan's career. Others opted for training in the chivalric code of knights.

As education was emphasized and developed, the church left a lasting influence based on the teaching and ministry of Jesus.

THE IMPACT OF JESUS ON LITERATURE

The literature of medieval times reflects the morals and teaching of Jesus. Most writers filled their work with Christian assumptions.

Much of the conventional literature was theological poetry, drama, and prose. The works written for the highly educated remained in Latin (in the West) and Greek (in the East). Some authors wrote in local languages if they designed their work for the masses.

The most educated people in the Middle Ages remained the monks; therefore, they became known as some of the greatest writers in the Middle Ages. Authors like Roger Bacon (c. 1220–1292) and Thomas Aquinas wrote on topics that explored a combination of Christian doctrine with other teachings.

Christian scholars and leaders supported (or at least allowed) secular literature, which also flourished during this time. Dramas, biographies, allegories, and satire entertained those who could read. Some writers focused on the retelling of mythological stories, most of which had their roots in Greek mythology. Heroic literature captured the period's emphasis on chivalric deeds and ideals of those heroes.

Dante Alighieri (1265–1321) is probably best known for his *Inferno*, part of *The Divine Comedy*, which many consider as one of the greatest works of classic literature. It provides

Christian Writers in the High Middle Ages

Although a monk, Thomas Aquinas remains best known for writing about philosophy. He revived much of Aristotle's teachings, combining them with Christianity in his philosophical works.

Roger Bacon's greatest work, *Opus Majus*, deals with areas of natural science. Written at the request of Pope Clement IV (1190/1200 1268), this 840-page work covers a broad range of subjects, including grammar, logic, mathematics, physics, and philosophy. Although he was a Benedictine friar, Bacon's studies led him far beyond the Bible, as seen in this classic work.

Painting of Dante Alighieri, which resides in the Cathedral of Saint Mary of the Flower (the Florence Cathedral), Italy

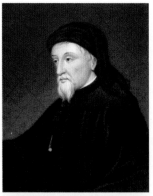
Geoffrey Chaucer

an excellent example of the attitudes and views of Christians during the Late Middle Ages. Dante dealt with many topics in the book, including heaven and hell.

Also during this era, Geoffrey Chaucer (c. 1343–1400) wrote *The Canterbury Tales* in Middle English. His work gave legitimacy to English as a language and earned him the title Father of English Literature. While a secular work, *The Canterbury Tales* reflects the influences of the church in society. Chaucer highlighted problems in the church, most especially regarding the selling of indulgences. Although he did not discuss the doctrine of indulgences, he explained how some people abused their positions through the sale of them.

THE IMPACT OF JESUS ON THE GOVERNMENT AND HUMAN RIGHTS

Gods and Kings

Throughout history, monarchies were commonplace. Depending on the culture, kings held their position either through maintaining fear in the population or by convincing the people that they had a divine right to rule. In some ancient cultures, the king was looked at as a god, so rebellion against him would equal rebellion against the gods and lead to catastrophic results. In Europe, a king was believed to receive his right to rule from God Himself and, in essence, sat upon the throne as Jesus Christ's surrogate.

In the power vacuum created by the fall of the Roman Empire, Europe broke into fiefdoms. Without an emperor, there was no central political power over Western Europe except for the pope of Rome. Although the pope was not considered the leader of any individual country, he did enjoy great power as a political and spiritual leader—even crowning and deposing kings.

The popes secured their power by controlling who could partake in the Eucharist. Within the tenets of the Roman Catholic Church, nobody could attain eternal life if they did not partake of the church's sacraments. Because of this, the fear of excommunication—and the resulting condemnation to hell—kept political leaders subservient to the pope. If a political leader wanted peace, he had to bend to the will of the church; otherwise the people would not have access to the sacraments and would revolt in favor of the church.

When King Philip Augustus of France (1165–1223) left his second wife and took a third, the pope ordered him to return to his second wife. King Philip refused this intrusion. In response, in AD 1200 the pope imposed an interdict on France to which King Philip submitted nine months later.

When Pope Innocent III sent Stephen Langton (c.1150–1228) in June of AD 1206 to serve as archbishop of Canterbury, King John of England (c. 1167–1216) refused to accept him. The pope excommunicated the king in AD 1209 and formerly deposed him. John responded by submitting to the authority of the pope, who restored the king to his throne.

In both of these cases, popes forced kings—who feared losing their thrones—to submit to the church's authority. While the king was a supreme ruler, without the support of the nobles and peasants, he could quickly lose his kingdom. Fear of losing their salvation was enough to cause the nobles, as well as the masses, to choose loyalties with the pope over their kings.

Stephen Langton versus The Monarchy

Stephen Langton, the archbishop of Canterbury, was a political scholar. He believed that kings tended to rule oppressively and ignore the law due to the total power they held over the people's lives. He also believed that subjects of the king should have the right to disobey the king if the commands of the king were unlawful. While never advocating open rebellion, Langton did believe in limiting the power of the throne. He publically disagreed with King John over just and unjust edicts.

Langton and the pope both understood the king's power. When King John refused to accept Langton as archbishop, Langton and the majority of the bishops left England for France, leaving the nation without spiritual leadership. This spiritual vacuum placed tremendous fear in the hearts of the people, as well as immense pressure on King John. When King John relented and submitted to the church, the clergy returned to England.

Stephen Langton, one of seventeen life-size statues representing the signatories of the Magna Carta, currently in the Canterbury Heritage Museum

THE MAGNA CARTA

As King John was sparring with the archbishop over the limits of royal authority, England was embroiled in an unsuccessful war with France. Rather than honor the long tradition of consulting with his barons regarding raising taxes and conscripting men for military service, the king acted independently and without their support. The English nobility felt slighted, which affected their loyalty to the king.

Langton, the bishops, and the barons worked out a peaceful settlement with the king, which would become the Magna Carta, a document that limited the king's authority to act outside the law. Specifically, it required that King John proclaim certain inalienable liberties and that his will not remain arbitrary in the case of free people.

King John signed the Magna Carta in 1215 under duress. He appealed to the pope for an annulment of the document, which the pope granted as a favor

Illustration of the Magna Carta being signed by King John, by John Leech (1817–1864)

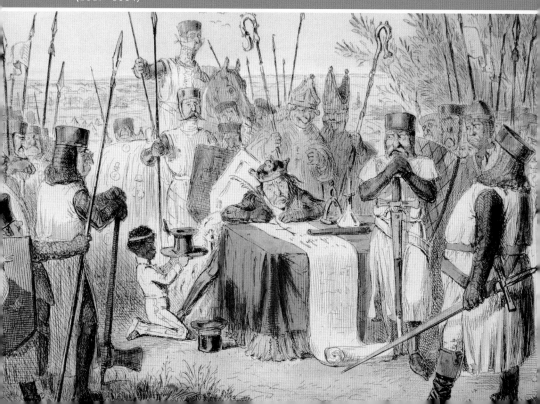

Magna Carta of King John, AD 1215

The Magna Carta, an English legal charter that required King John of England to acknowledge the rights and freedom of his subjects

in response to King John's newly placed loyalty. However, that was not the end of the Magna Carta; it was reissued in 1216, 1217, and 1225. However, it was not until 1297 that the final version of the Magna Carta was signed and implemented as law.

The Magna Carta, one of the most important legal documents of history, promoted the Christian concepts of liberty and justice. It was later held up as part of the English common law, which ruled over the kings of England. Ultimately, it became part of the foundation of both English and American law, promoting the freedom taught by Jesus and the church that followed.

The Magna Carta and Jesus

The Magna Carta has strong Christian ties. It stands as the first political document to recognize that Christ's teaching on freedom applies to the political realm as well as to the spiritual one. The preamble leaves no doubt that it was inspired by Jesus Christ: "Out of reverence for God and for the salvation of our soul and those of our ancestors and heirs, for the honor of God and the exaltation of Holy Church and the reform of our realm, on the advice of our revered fathers."

THE IMPACT OF JESUS ON ART

Most medieval art contained Christian subjects because the church commissioned more artwork than anyone else. As a result, churches and cathedrals across Europe house the works of masters like Michelangelo (1475–1564), Rembrandt (1606–1669), and Vermeer (1632–1675).

Mosaic of Jesus in the Hagia Sophia, currently a museum in Istanbul, Turkey

Ceiling of the Sistine Chapel in the Vatican (Italy), featuring Michelangelo's paintings

Illuminated manuscripts and mosaics were also enjoyed during this period. Highly ornate metalwork in gold and silver was used for most of the vessels employed in the Mass. Gold chalices with embedded gems were used for the wine during the communion service.

Some of the artwork became part of the church's architecture through *frescoes*. (A fresco is painted into wet lime plaster, making it an integral part of the building. The "paint" is pure pigment in a water base. This technique provides vibrant, permanent colors for the artists to use.) Painting these masterpieces as frescoes has allowed many of them to survive through the centuries. During a recent restoration of Leonardo da Vinci's (1452–1519) *Last Supper*, workers found that the artist's original colors were much more vibrant than those used in previous restoration work.

In addition to paintings, many artists developed sculptures. Michelangelo's *David*, a lifelike marble statue, appears as if it will walk off its base at any moment.

The Creation of Adam, Michelangelo (1475–1564)

The style and use of art in the Eastern and Western churches was quite different. The Eastern church's art focused mostly on icons of biblical personalities and saints, while the Western church depicted famous scenes, such as da Vinci's *Last Supper* and Michelangelo's paintings within the Sistine Chapel.

The Origin of Art

Ever since the dawn of time, humanity has used art as expression and also as worship. Tubal-Cain, a mere six generations from Cain, was the first artist mentioned in the Bible, working in brass and iron (Genesis 4:22). Like him, many ancient people adorned their everyday tools and utensils, personalizing them and expressing their innate creativity. Nowhere do we find greater examples of this ancient art than in the religious objects created by these people.

When God commanded Moses to build and decorate the tabernacle, He specifically called out Bezalel. God commissioned this artisan to complete the furnishings of the tabernacle, divinely inspiring the work (Exodus 31:2–5). He also singled out Oholiab to help Bezalel (Exodus 31:6).

Wealthy patrons also commissioned artists to paint portraits, and the artistic interests of Rembrandt, Vermeer, and others encouraged painting scenes that depicted everyday life, capturing the Middle Ages in images.

Islamic artists also began to flourish in the East. Because the Muslim faith discourages the creation of images of people, many of the great Islamic artists of this period displayed mastery of geometric and foliage patterns.

ICONOGRAPHY AND ICONOCLASTS

The sacred images representing the saints, the Virgin, and Jesus Christ

Mosaic of the holy family at the entrance of Saint Mark's Basilica in Venice, Italy

inspired great thoughts and worship in the Eastern church. However, opposing views about the appropriate use of icons created points of dispute between the Eastern and Western churches. While believers didn't pray to the icon itself, the icon offered a mental image of the object of their prayers, allowing them to focus their prayers more specifically. It was believed that this ability to focus helped ensure prayers went directly to the appropriate saint or to Christ. To the Orthodox believer, the presence of icons offered reminders of the ongoing presence of Jesus Christ and the saints.

God's View of Art

God created art for His use and His glory. While there have been those who disagreed with the use of art in the church, seeing it as a form of idolatry, artwork existed in the Hebrew tabernacle because God commanded it. The adornment of cathedrals and basilicas during the High Middle Ages was merely an extension of this commandment.

The Madonna with Child, icon in Saint Willibrordus Church, Antwerp, Belgium

In 726, Byzantine emperor Leo III declared that these images were idols and forbade their use. In addition to the potential for idolatry, he was concerned that Jews and Muslims would see the icons as "graven images" impeding their conversion to Christ. His edict demanded their destruction wherever found.

The debate in the West about the use of icons waxed and waned through the centuries, depending on who was emperor of Rome at the time. Iconoclasm (the destruction of images) was revived under the Byzantine emperor Leo V during the papacy of Paschal I. Paschal intervened but was unsuccessful.

THE IMPACT OF JESUS ON MEDICINE AND CARE OF THE SICK

Beginning with the plagues in the Roman Empire during the early years of the church, Christians took special concern for the sick. During the Plague of Cyprian in Alexandria, Egypt (North Africa), Christians became the

principal caregivers for the ill. The same happened during the Antonine Plague in the unified Roman Empire and the Plague of Justinian in the Byzantine Empire. Because of their concern for the sick, Christians created hospitals to offer hospitality and care to those who were sick.

Charlemagne called for the restoration of hospitals that had been functioning before he came to power but that had deteriorated. With a desire to meet physical and spiritual needs, Charlemagne required that hospitals and monasteries work together. This work was often undertaken by widows, deaconesses, and virgins who received payment by the church to serve as nurses. As time went on, monks and nuns became the primary caregivers. Christianity had an impact on the care of the sick and the development of hospitals; by the tenth century, monasteries throughout Europe had become the dominant force in hospital care. (Hospitals had existed earlier in the Roman Empire but were limited by serving a special interest, such as soldiers, slaves, or gladiators. Charlemagne's steps began to provide health care to the general population.)

As the Crusaders battled through the Middle East, trying to free Jerusalem from Muslim control, they built hospitals to care for those who became sick or injured along their way. These hospitals provided care for wounded soldiers, as well as people from surrounding communities. Christian advocacy for compassionate treatment of patients set the direction for hospitals throughout their history.

Many health care orders were founded during the times of the Crusades. These orders did not deny health care to anyone, Christian or Muslim. The Knights of the Order of Hospitallers of St. John of Jerusalem built a hospital in Jerusalem. Although cynics may view the development of hospitals as the result of misguided crusades, these institutions created a lasting presence to care for the sick and the poor.

Christianity and the Black Death

Christian health care was at the forefront of battling the Black Death. Due to the high number of victims and the rapid spread of the disease, many health care workers fled the hospitals in fear. Yet, nuns and friars in Paris (fourteenth century) stayed by the bedsides of their patients, showing compassion to those who were suffering, even at great risk to their own lives.

Guy de Chauliac (c. 1300–1368), a cleric and surgeon in Avignon, stayed to serve while others were fleeing. During the plague, he made significant observations about how the epidemic was affecting people, and he experimented with different treatment methods.

Hôtel-Dieu Hospital at sunrise in Paris, where many patients with the Black Death were treated in the fourteenth century

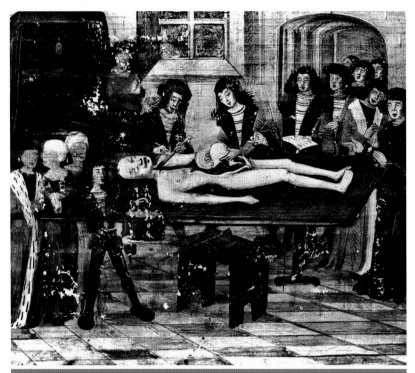

Guy de Chauliac, a French physician and surgeon, treated patients with the plague. Here Chauliac gives an anatomy lesson.

Christ's influence was strong in the care of the sick. In the years He walked upon the earth, He healed countless people. He was always ready to reach a hand out to help the sick. Jesus' compassion overcame Jewish tradition, cultural laws, and prevailing wisdom as He extended His hands even to lepers, which was forbidden by Old Testament law. Christians throughout history have followed the example of Jesus, putting their lives at risk to serve the needs of those suffering from plagues and infirmities.

Hospitals became commonplace throughout Europe. England may have housed as many as six hundred hospitals in the fourteenth century. The local residents of the time often referred to a hospital as "God's House" to acknowledge God's healing intervention.

Toward the end of the Middle Ages, hospitals became secularized. Nevertheless, the example of the church inspired nearly a thousand years of hospital care. The church also preserved many medical texts. Even during the Dark

Ages of Europe, monks worked to copy and preserve these documents. Christian universities also taught medicine, advancing the knowledge of health care and improving its quality.

As the secular world gradually took over the running of hospitals, there were some sick people that were denied care. Hospital workers often shunned lepers and others with communicable diseases. The Christian churches, however, continued to assist even these patients.

THE IMPACT OF JESUS ON EXPLORATION

The early Roman Empire existed during a time of exploration. The Romans sought to conquer and bring new people under the umbrella of the empire. This exploration stopped when pressures caused the empire to split into East and West, which led to a tumultuous time period known as the Dark Ages. After the Crusades, however, exploration efforts began anew. While the

The Landing of Columbus in the New World, Currier & Ives (1846)

Christopher means "Christ bearer." Columbus signed his name Xpo FERENS (*X* referred to the cross, and *Ferens* is Latin for "bearer").

debate among historians remains inconclusive, most believe that the outward focus and expansion that developed during the Crusades may have rekindled interest in exploration.

While fame and financial gain were prime motivators for the explorers, some in the Christian faith saw a new opportunity to heed Christ's great commission and spread the gospel to foreign lands. Even journeys motivated by financial gain included priests, who ministered to the sailors and worked as missionaries in the lands they visited.

Christopher Columbus's (c. 1451–1506) spirit of exploration was twofold. While his primary motivation may have been financial (or perhaps a sense of adventure), he also aimed to spread the message of Jesus Christ throughout his journey. In his first report to King Ferdinand (1452–1516) and Queen Isabella (1451–1504) of Spain, he stated that he "wanted to be true to Christ's command."[4] As he explored, he left crosses wherever he touched land and named his first landfall *San Salvador* (which means "Holy Savior").

Columbus's journals contain many references to God. Columbus thanked Him for His providence and spoke of God's blessings. Although Columbus failed to treat the people in the New World with Christ's perfect love, the salvation of souls motivated him. He wrote, "Let Christ rejoice on earth, as

Henry the Navigator on Discovery Monument (Lisbon, Portugal)

He rejoices in heaven in the prospect of the salvation of the souls of so many nations hitherto lost."[5]

Another explorer, Henry the Navigator (1394–1460), of the Portuguese Order of Christ, sponsored voyages with the intent of opening trade routes, discovering the extent of Islam, and spreading the Christian faith. The Order of Christ provided funding for some of his travels, with the understanding that his priorities would aid the conversion of heathens to Christianity and inflict damage on Islamic territories.

Portugal and Spain stood at the forefront of exploration. These two countries opened trade routes to India and the Far East, bringing monks and priests to establish missions aimed at converting the people to Christ. Their overseas competition was so fierce that it caused Pope Alexander VI to sign a papal bull, creating the Treaty of Tordesillas. According to this treaty, non-Christian lands one hundred leagues west and south of the Azores or the Cape Verde Islands would belong to Spain, and non-Christian lands east of that line would belong to Portugal.

This treaty ignored Muslim traders and explorers, who were equally active in the Far East. Disputes arose between Spain and Portugal and the Muslims, often leading to bloodshed. In one case, the Portuguese explorer Vasco da Gama (c. 1460–1524) is said to have captured a Muslim boat with over two

Hernán Cortés

Was Hernán Cortés a hero or a villain?

The Case for Hero: Cortés introduced the gospel to the New World and oversaw the widespread expansion of the church. He confronted and stopped the practice of infant sacrifice and established hospitals. He abhorred the cannibalism he discovered and believed that introducing Christianity to the people would replace such practices with the love of Christ.

The Case for Villain: The accomplishments of Cortés came at the cost of over 200,000 lives. While he advanced the gospel in ways that fit the cultural expectation of his day, his violent methods of conversion fought the standard of Christ he claimed to bear.

hundred Muslim men, women, and children on it. He burned the ship to the waterline, killing nearly everyone aboard.

While the spreading of the gospel may have been one of the stated reasons for these explorations, the combination of sharing the gospel and seeking earthly gains resulted in predictable failures. Indeed, the greedy character of those who undertook spreading the gospel tainted the message and its legacy.

Similarly, the Spanish and Portuguese conquistadores invaded the New World during the fifteenth and sixteenth centuries. These were military men sent on a quest that combined military conquest, acquisition of riches, and Christian evangelism. Their cruel methods forcibly converted most of the Americas—from Mexico south to Argentina—to Catholic Christianity. Some reports say that the Franciscan monks who traveled with the conquistador Hernán Cortés (1485–1547) baptized over five million Aztec, Mayan, and Zapotec Indians.

While the conquistadores were cruel and motivated by financial gain, Christianity arrived in the Americas and secured a permanent presence. Despite bad behavior and bloodshed, the teaching of Jesus has thrived in the Western Hemisphere.

From the beginning of the church, devoted followers of Jesus Christ have aspired to spread the gospel. And while we know the work as *missions* today, the word wasn't used until the early 1400s. Before then, evangelists called their work many things: "proclaiming the gospel," "preaching to the people,"

Illustration of Franciscans of the California missions in *San Juan Capistrano Mission* by Zephyrin Engelhardt (1851–1934)

"propagation of the faith," and simply "gospel work." Missions referred to both the work done among the people and the geographical areas that needed the gospel. Although not a biblical term, *missions* has defined this aspect of Christian work for over five hundred years.

Crusaders and conquistadores imperfectly spread the gospel of Jesus Christ, often putting fighting before evangelism, decrying the message of Christ and His love. The resulting trade routes became routes for the gospel, with groups being funded and commissioned directly by the pope to Africa, Asia, and the Americas.

Missions work in the latter Middle Ages owes much to the religious orders that undertook this work. Most prominently, Franciscan and Dominican monks took up the call for missions. Their study and training, as well as their ascetic lifestyle, made them ideal missionaries. Many thousands answered the call, some knowing they would likely die spreading the gospel.

Jesus' Impact: Missions

He said to them, "Go into all the world and preach the gospel to all creation. Whoever believes and is baptized will be saved, but whoever does not believe will be condemned." (Mark 16:15–16)

These missions efforts started in Africa, long before moving to Asia or the Americas. Christianity in Africa began in Ethiopia in the fourth century. People in the Nubian Kingdom, just south of Egypt, converted to Christ around AD 540, if not earlier.

The message of Christ resonated well with African leaders, as the values of Christianity appealed to them. Various African tribes readily accepted the teachings of Jesus, as they were people who understood covenants and their worldview predisposed them to the message of Christ. Because these were tribal communities, when one leader would convert, it was not uncommon for the entire tribe to convert.

Because the inland African church was largely cut off from the rest of Christendom, it did not have the leadership to sustain itself once the missionaries died. Few natives were trained to take the place of missionary leaders within the African church. They also lacked proper representation in Rome. In many cases, people groups who converted to Christ later fell to Islamic expansion.

Archaeological records show that Christianity made inroads into China during the Tang Dynasty in the seventh century. During that time, the emperor of

China deemed Christianity beneficial to the Chinese people and allowed their access to it. However, this favor did not continue. In 845, the new emperor, Wuzong (814–846), banned all foreign religions.

Around the same time, Muslims shut down the Silk Road to China, blocking efforts to sustain the church there. After the Mongol invasion, four hundred years later, the pope commissioned missionaries and sent them to China. The missionaries to this new frontier included Franciscan monk Giovanni da Montecorvino (1247–1328), who went to the capital of China in 1294. Finding the Mongol emperor tolerant of various religions, Giovanni built a number of churches and converted at least six thousand Chinese and Mongols to the gospel of Christ.

The renewed missionary gains by the church in China were short-lived. The harsh treatment of the Mongols toward the Chinese created resentment, leading to a Chinese rebellion. At the same time, Islam made inroads into the Mongol people, converting some leaders. This combination of events caused the decline of the church in China.

CHRISTENDOM AND CULTURE

Unlike during the time of the Roman Empire, Europe didn't have a central political identity during the latter Middle Ages. The people of Europe identified themselves as being part of *Christendom*. This term—roughly analogous to a "kingdom"—showed the influence of Christianity on European society.

Image from an unknown artist revealing the tripartite social order of the Middle Ages: cleric (those who pray); knight (those who fight); and workman (those who work)

Everywhere Christians lived was part of Christendom. This label wasn't tied to borders or regions and had nothing to do with geography. More than anything, Christendom was an ideal and a way of life. Christians firmly believed that Jesus Christ and His teachings impacted every area of their lives and

Engraving by Bocquet of Henry IV, published in the *Catalogue of the Royal and Noble Authors*, United Kingdom (1806)

their world. Jesus did not intend His teaching to be locked inside the doors of the church but offered applications for every aspect of daily life. He expected His followers to use their faith as a guide for everyday activities.

During the early Middle Ages, the church was the major unifying force in Western Europe. When the government was weak and disorganized, the church provided organization and direction for society. Since Christendom was secular as well as spiritual, the papacy often assumed control of temporal issues as well as spiritual ones. With the monasteries serving as an integral part of education and health care, the church had a continual involvement in many government and social functions. The church's influence extended as far as military matters; it was the popes who called for and commissioned knights and soldiers to go on the Crusades.

As during the Roman Empire, the marriage of church and individual states created ongoing problems. There were constant power struggles between secular rulers and the pope. Popes, kings, and emperors clashed over claims of ultimate authority.

Pope Gregory VII (c. 1015/1028–1085) believed in the pope's superiority over secular rulers. This belief

Relations Between Henry IV and Pope Gregory VII

The disagreement between Henry IV and Pope Gregory VII became so severe that the pope threatened to excommunicate Henry. In response, Henry convened his national council in Worms, Germany, and deposed the pope. In return, the pope excommunicated Henry and freed his people from their allegiance to the king.

Pressure from the princes of Germany forced Henry to seek absolution and reconciliation with Gregory. Although Gregory tried to avoid Henry, the emperor forced the issue by performing public penance before him. After prolonged negotiations, reconciliation was reached.

was reflected in a bizarre document known as the *Dictatus Papae*, which included the unheard of claim "that he [the Pope] may depose emperors."[6] Emperor Henry IV (1050–1106) took issue with the pope's declaration but temporarily submitted to him to receive the church's support in his war against the Saxons. Once he had victory, he then returned to his dispute with the pope, specifically in reestablishing political ties with excommunicated nobles. He also promoted the archbishop of Milan, usurping the pope's right to appoint bishops and archbishops.

Struggles like the one between Henry IV and Gregory VII were not uncommon, as the only actual power the papacy had over secular rulers was that of excommunication. As nationalism grew, along with alliances between various kingdoms, the church lost much of its influence over people's lives. However, the church still functioned as a unifying religious force, holding the people of the various nations together.

Stained-glass artwork of Saint Francis of Assisi in the Church of Saint James the Greater, Elba, Italy

FRANCIS OF ASSISI

Francis of Assisi (c. 1181–1226) was born to a wealthy family of Italian silk merchants. As a young man, he left school by the age of fourteen, often drank, socialized heavily, and created trouble. Francis served in the army of Assisi but was captured in a battle between Assisi and Perugia.

The army of Perugia held Francis as a prisoner for almost a year while awaiting ransom, a common tactic when noblemen and the wealthy were captured in battle. It was during this time of captivity that he began seeing visions. Returning to Assisi, he heard the voice of Jesus telling him to repair the

Christian church. Leaving his worldly life behind, he dedicated himself to poverty and service to Christ.

At first, Francis understood the words he had received to mean that he must physically repair the broken down churches and chapels. While engaged in this work, he heard a sermon on Matthew 10:9–15, where Jesus told His disciples to go forth and proclaim the kingdom of heaven. He was touched by the command to not take money, a walking stick, or extra clothes. In this, he saw his life's calling.

The Dream of Innocent III, Giotto di Bondone (c. 1266–1337). Saint Francis of Assisi is seen in this legendary dream as carrying the church.

Although Francis declined ordination as a priest, he began preaching repentance. Gradually, he gathered followers, who lived together as "lesser brothers." After a year, he traveled to Rome, taking his first dozen converts with him. There he sought permission from Pope Innocent III to start a new religious order. In April of 1210, the pope approved. This led to the official founding of the Franciscan Order, more commonly known as the Friars Minor. Later Francis added a women's order (known as the Order of Poor Clares) and eventually a third order (known as the Order of Brothers and Sisters of Penance).

The Franciscan Order required a commitment to personal poverty. Francis himself renounced his family and claim to his inheritance. He and his followers lived a simple life and preached on the streets wherever they could find an audience.

Franciscan friars traveled extensively, teaching in Italy, Spain, Tunisia, Morocco, Hungary, and France. A group visited China as Ambassadors of Peace and Faith. They translated the New Testament and the book of Psalms into the common Chinese vernacular, but the Chinese leaders and people rejected their foreign doctrine.

Francis himself traveled to Egypt to try to convert an Egyptian sultan, a nephew of Saladin, the Muslim ruler. At the time, the Sultan al-Kamil was in Damietta, located on one of the tributaries of the Nile. During a four-week cease-fire, Francis and his companions were able to cross the lines and preach to the Muslims in the city.

THE IMPACT OF JESUS ON LINGUISTICS

As the church sent out missionaries, the need for language training became evident. The Dominican and Franciscan Orders became the first to study languages, allowing them to preach to people in their own languages. While the monks studied many different languages, the Crusades made it necessary for them to study Arabic, Hebrew, and Syrian.

Learning the languages of the Muslims allowed the monks to read and study the sciences and philosophy furthered by the Muslims in the Holy Land. As the foremost preservers of knowledge during this time, the monks would combine studies with missions work, copying texts and sending them back to their monasteries' libraries.

These panels show three important episodes in Llull's life: the vision he saw of Christ on the cross, which led to his conversion (left); his pilgrimmage to Saint Mary of Rocamadour (middle); and his interview with Raymond of Peñafort in Barcelona (right), who may have influenced Llull in his work with Muslims. From *Life of Raymond Lull,* a fourteenth-century manuscript by an unknown artist.

One of the greatest Christian scholars of Islam during this time was Ramon Llull (c. 1232–1315), a Franciscan of the Third Order. He studied Arabic and devoted himself to learning all he could about the culture and customs of Islam. He dedicated nine years to studying their culture, philosophy, and religion. His goal was to speak in the people's own language in order to convert and unite humanity through the power of Christ's love.

In 1276, Pope John XXI (c. 1215–1277) gave Llull permission to open a language school in the Monastery of Miramar. The school was the first of its kind and provided formal training to friars who would live in Muslim lands.

Ramon Llull and Muslims

A story has it that Llull learned an important lesson from a Muslim slave who taught him about Muslim culture in an unexpected way. When the slave blasphemed Christ, Llull became angry and struck the slave. The slave pulled a knife in response, for which he was imprisoned.

The slave committed suicide in jail, which convicted Llull that the only way to win Muslims to Christ was through love, not force. The Muslims knew how to respond to violence, but they didn't know how to respond to love.

QUESTIONS

1. In what ways did lust for power cause the church to lose its sense of mission that the gospel provides?

2. In what ways did the Crusades serve righteous and unrighteous causes?

3. How did the cathedrals of the Middle Ages reveal the gospel to the people?

4. What were some of the contributions of monks and monasteries during this time?

5. What is the significance of the Magna Carta, as outlined in this chapter?

6. How did Christopher Columbus's blend of mission and business mirror other explorers of the time?

7. What is Christendom?

Chapter 5
THE IMPACT OF JESUS ON REFORM AND FREEDOM
(1400–1700)

The Roman Catholic Church in the Middle Ages boasted vast political power. However, this power came at a price: the more the church leaders embroiled themselves in politics, the more secularized they became. They increasingly placed their faith in political power rather than in the power of the cross. But as Europe moved into the Renaissance, the church's political power began to change.

Painting in Saint Salvator's Cathedral, Bruges, Belgium

Engraving from 1881 of Johannes Gutenberg (right) and his printing press

THE IMPACT OF JESUS ON THE SPREAD OF IDEAS THROUGH PRINTING

Before Johannes Gutenberg (c. 1395–1468) developed the movable type press, printing was laborious, unreliable, and expensive. Each page had to be hand carved in reverse into a wood block. Because of the extensive labor needed to carve each block, few people ever printed books.

After seeing the impact his work could have on spreading the gospel, Gutenberg reflected:

> God suffers in the multitude of souls whom His word can not reach. Religious truth is imprisoned in a small number of manuscript books which confine instead of spread the public treasure. Let us break the seal which seals up holy things and give wings to Truth in order that

The Gutenberg Bible, the first book printed in the West using movable type

she may win every soul that comes into the world by her word no longer written at great expense by hands easily palsied, but multiplied like the wind by an untiring machine.[1]

Gutenberg's invention coincided with an increase in the availability of paper, as the Muslims had started to manufacture it in Europe. Paper was much cheaper than vellum and parchment, making it ideal for use with Gutenberg's press. Eleven years after the movable press was invented, Gutenberg published his first book: the Bible. For the first time in history, the Bible became available for widespread public reading.

Because education expanded in Europe and literacy rates grew tremendously in the fourteenth and fifteenth centuries, newly published Bibles found new homes. Before Gutenberg's innovation, only the upper class and residents of monasteries read; now—over time—a larger population found new interest in reading.

Printing the Bible helped launch the church's reformation in an unexpected way. As copies of the Bible became more widely available, readers began to notice discrepancies in the church's handwritten copies. Early textual critics began to question the Bible's accuracy and the church's teaching. Some scholars began to seek out the best Hebrew and Greek copies of the Bible. Scholars assembled more accurate Bible manuscripts and developed a hunger to seek truth rather than blindly accept church dogma. This became the first step toward the *Textus Receptus*, which became an established standard version of the New Testament in its original Greek language.

Martin Luther (1483–1546), a prolific writer, was one of the early monks who sought out original Greek and Hebrew texts in order to discover the truth

Martin Luther. Originally published between 1905 and 1909. Artist unknown.

of God's Word. His articles, pamphlets, and books gained a wide audience because of new printing technologies.

Luther taught that salvation came through faith in Jesus Christ alone; he condemned the church's collection of indulgences and other corruption. He challenged people to study the Bible for themselves instead of unquestioningly accepting the church's message. He encouraged individuals to follow Jesus and His teaching rather than tradition and dogma.

THE IMPACT OF JESUS ON THE PRESERVATION OF THE HEBREW AND GREEK LANGUAGES

It was primarily faith in Jesus Christ that drove Christian scholars to preserve and print Bible manuscripts in their original languages. But as printed Bibles became more widespread, students discovered a growing number of transcription errors made by those who had hand copied Bibles throughout the centuries. Skilled Bible students began to improve Greek and Hebrew manuscripts so that the new copies were consistent with each other.

With a newly discovered hunger to study biblical texts in the original languages, many scholars began to learn Greek and Hebrew. Martin Luther described this desire extremely well:

> If I were younger I would want to learn this language [Hebrew], for without it one can never properly understand the Holy Scripture . . . .The Jews drink out of the original spring, The Greeks drink out of the stream flowing out of the spring; the Latins, however, out of the puddle. . .without knowledge of Hebrew and Greek, preaching is flat and tame; men grow at last wearied and disgusted and it falls to the ground.[2]

At the center of Hebrew and Greek study was a humanist[3] scholar named Johannes Reuchlin (1455–1522). Likely the greatest European Hebrew scholar of his time, Reuchlin wrote a Hebrew grammar and taught others the original biblical languages. Efforts like his furthered the study of scripture, which became an important component of the Reformation.

Another strong proponent of studying the original biblical languages was a Catholic priest named Erasmus (c. 1466–1536). A theologian and humanist, Erasmus actively fought critics who insisted that only Latin was suitable for the scriptures.[4] He also prepared the first Greek New Testament for publication. His Greek work encouraged further translations of the Bible into the various vernaculars of the people of Europe.

Portrait of Desiderius Erasmus of Rotterdam with the Renaissance Pilaster, Hans Holbein the Younger (c. 1498–1543)

Erasmus's desire to empower the people to study the Sacred Scriptures in their own language shows clearly in his statement:

> Do we desire to learn, is there then any authority better than Christ? We read and reread the works of a friend, but there are thousands of Christians who have never read the gospels and the epistles in all their lives. The Mohammedans study the

Example of a Hebrew Torah, written on goat skin parchment by a trained scribe with a feather quill

Koran, the Jews peruse Moses. Why do we not the same for Christ? He is our only doctor.[5]

Elsewhere in Europe, Oxford professor John Colet (1467–1519) started reading the New Testament in Greek and translating it into English in 1496. His desire for the people to understand the gospel led him to share these readings with his students and later, due to their popularity, with the public at St. Paul's Cathedral. His public presentations of the New Testament in English became so popular that they drew audiences that numbered in the thousands.

THE IMPACT OF JESUS ON LITERACY

While the church during this time believed the scriptures were their source for authority, they also believed that only those trained to read the scriptures correctly should do so. Because the church insisted that proper training existed only with priests and church officials, laypeople were forbidden from reading the Bible for themselves—priests interpreted the Bible for them.

Following church tradition, many priests focused their teaching on church dogma rather than on the scriptures themselves.

Because the church stood between its parishioners and the Bible, Reformers such as Martin Luther, John Calvin (1509–1564), and John Wycliffe (c. 1331–1384) worked to make the Bible available to everyone in their own language. Luther believed that the only way for God to communicate with humanity was through His written Word. Luther believed, "Christ is the essence of Scripture and in Christ the Word became flesh." [6]

The Septuagint

The historical Greek translation of the Old Testament is called the *Septuagint.* Originally translated from Hebrew to Greek, this classic version of the Old Testament once enjoyed widespread use among the Jewish people who lived during the times of Jesus and Paul. Because of the church's insistence on Latin, monks had abandoned the Septuagint and copied only Latin versions. By the Renaissance, very few copies of the Septuagint existed in Europe.

Reading among commoners continued to increase. Ordinary people attained a taste for the growing number of published books and developed an interest in reading the Bible for themselves. As a result, the Reformation contributed to both increased literacy and the efforts to translate the Bible.

This emphasis on reading helped propel a new movement of literacy. The public's interest in education drove governments to create tax-funded education efforts that began to replace the church's education model. As a growing number of people became better educated, economies in Europe became more robust as a new class of businesspeople opened storefronts

Stained glass from Wycliffe College Chapel, Toronto (2007)

and developed cottage industries. The desire to read of Jesus and His teaching was a contributing factor to the material prosperity throughout Europe.

THE IMPACT OF JESUS ON GOVERNMENT AND SOCIETY

The increase in education gave many people opportunities their ancestors did not have. Those who worked hard had a chance to improve their financial standing. A middle class began to emerge. People found new opportunities, and cities began to grow.

While the Reformation was a religious movement, it also contributed to a transformation in society as a whole. For the first time in their generation, people discovered that having a harder work ethic often translated into discovering better opportunities. More and more ordinary people began to develop a personal work ethic; they began to work for their own benefit—not that of a ruling lord. And while they took ownership to improve their financial well-being, they also took responsibility for their own faith and spiritual development. The church still held importance, but it was not the end-all means of spiritual awareness and growth.

The earliest Reformers didn't seek to fundamentally change culture or separate the church from the state. In fact, many of them thought the church should be involved in government and that the government should integrate at some level with the church. For most, their primary effort was to restore the scriptural roots of the church.

Because the Western church and state were so closely intertwined, the church's Reformers impacted society as well. As they worked to bring the church back to Jesus, the teachings of Jesus began to touch every area of daily life.

The Effect of Bible Translation

Brave Christians undertook translation efforts during this time. John Wycliffe translated the Bible into English. Martin Luther translated the New Testament into German in 1522, and Jacob Lefevre translated it into French later that same decade. Each translation engaged an eager audience among the lower class.

The Bible's production in France found an enthusiastic audience with the Huguenots.[7] This educated class expanded their desire to read the Bible and wanted to transform the church so laypeople could discover Jesus Christ for themselves and read the words He spoke. They believed they could deepen their faith through personal biblical studies. Their studies encouraged them to demand changes in church practices and question accepted cultural values, such as the divine right of a king to rule.

Luther and the other Reformers placed a high value on hard work. They believed that work was pleasing to God and that each and every occupation could be a spiritual vocation if done for the glory of God. Work had a spiritual purpose beyond mere survival.

Luther

Born in Germany in 1483, Martin Luther became a Catholic monk in the Augustinian Order. Through his own struggles with biblical understanding, he became convinced that God justified His followers solely through their

Engraving of John Wycliffe by J. Posselwhite, United Kingdom (1833)

act of faith and not by church sacrament. His Ninety-Five Theses, which he allegedly nailed to the castle church door in Wittenberg on October 31, 1517, are widely recognized as the spark that started the Reformation. And while they did launch a public debate, Luther's impact also benefited from the timing of a culture that was growing eager for change.

Luther confronted the Roman Catholic Church on several issues, but he did not initially set out to oppose the pope. Rather, Luther believed that people around the pope had twisted the pontiff's will. Chief among Luther's complaints was the sale of indulgences to reduce a dead soul's time in Purgatory.

Luther's conflict with the established church continued to escalate until he faced a spiritual crisis in 1519. Because he became loudly outspoken against many of the excesses of the church and the materialism in

Jesus' Impact:
The Bible's Life-Giving Message

"And the Father who sent me has himself testified concerning me. You have never heard his voice nor seen his form, nor does his word dwell in you, for you do not believe the one he sent. You study the Scriptures diligently because you think that in them you have eternal life. These are the very Scriptures that testify about me, yet you refuse to come to me to have life." (John 5:37–40)

Painting by Pieter Brueghel II (c. 1564–1636) of medieval life

church leadership, he faced excommunication. Luther had to choose between church tradition and his devotion to his views about the Bible. When faced with a papal bull threatening excommunication, he burned the order, denying the supremacy of the pope. At the Diet of Worms, he refused to recant from his preaching and written works and went into hiding.

While in hiding, Martin Luther translated the Bible into German so that the people could experience

Jesus' Impact:
Christian Work Ethic

"You are the light of the world. A town built on a hill cannot be hidden. Neither do people light a lamp and put it under a bowl. Instead they put it on its stand, and it gives light to everyone in the house. In the same way, let your light shine before others, that they may see your good deeds and glorify your Father in heaven." (Matthew 5:14–16)

God's Holy Word for themselves. He believed that God's primary method

Young Peasant with Sickle, Vincent van Gogh (1853–1890)

First public monument of reformer, monk, theologian, and Bible translator Martin Luther

of communication was His Word. As time went on, he became more confident in his beliefs, debating Erasmus (in person) and Calvin (through his writing). Luther centered his theology on three points: *sola scriptura* (scripture alone), *sola gratia* (grace alone), and *sola fide* (faith alone).

Müntzer

Thomas Müntzer (c. 1489–1525), another German Reformer, was a rebel leader during the Peasants' War (1524–1525). He publically criticized the sale of indulgences and sought a complete reformation of society on issues ranging from economics to civil government.

Jesus' Impact:
Justification through Faith Alone

Then he turned toward the woman and said to Simon, "Do you see this woman? . . . I tell you, her many sins have been forgiven— as her great love has shown. But whoever has been forgiven little loves little." Then Jesus said to her, "Your sins are forgiven." The other guests began to say among themselves, "Who is this who even forgives sins?" Jesus said to the woman, "Your faith has saved you; go in peace." (Luke 7:44–50)

Müntzer's ideas went beyond where Luther was comfortable; and while they each contributed to the Reformation, Luther refused to endorse Müntzer's more radical views. Müntzer was beheaded for his participation in the Peasants' War.

Calvin

A Frenchman born in 1509, John Calvin studied Luther's teachings and converted in 1533. Calvin was a strong defender of the Reformation, formally breaking with the Catholic Church. And although Calvin sought to shake off the shackles of the Roman Catholic Church, he also taught that all the citizens in town should be under the moral discipline of the church.

> **Predestination**
>
> Calvinism promotes the doctrine of predestination. This view is expressed in Calvin's own words: "We can only know God if He chooses to be known. Pardon and salvation are possible only through the free working of the grace of God. Before creation, God chose some of his creatures for salvation and others for destruction."[8]

THE IMPACT OF JESUS ON WAR

European residents during the Renaissance knew the effects of war. Since the fall of the Roman Empire, competing peoples and cultures often found themselves at odds. The spiritual reformers of the period generally advocated for peace.[9]

The Catholic Church of the time taught that the believer could pick up the sword in defense of home and country when necessary. In contrast, Martin Luther promoted that Christians should practice nonresistance at all times. (However, he also believed that as citizens, we have a duty to obey the law if we are called to fight by proper civil authority. While this may seem like a contradiction, it is important to remember that Luther believed in finding a balance between being a Christian and a responsible citizen of the state.)

> **Jesus' Impact: Peacemaking**
>
> "Peace I leave with you; my peace I give you. I do not give to you as the world gives. Do not let your hearts be troubled and do not be afraid." (John 14:27)

The Peasant War – Assembling, Constantin Meunier (1831–1905)

The issue of a Christian's place in war came to a head in Switzerland. The Swiss had a robust mercenary system in place. They had a reputation for being strong fighters. With the intense poverty that existed in Switzerland, sending young men off to war removed some of the financial burdens from the community while ensuring that those young men would be bringing foreign money home.

One of the greatest customers of these mercenary armies was the Vatican. For over five hundred years, the Vatican hired Swiss soldiers. The

Jesus' Impact:
The Doctrine of Predestination

"No one can come to me unless the Father who sent me draws them, and I will raise them up at the last day." (John 6:44)

"You did not choose me, but I chose you and appointed you so that you might go and bear fruit—fruit that will last—and so that whatever you ask in my name the Father will give you." (John 15:16)

Sculpture of Protestant Reformers William Farel, John Calvin, Theodore Beza, and John Knox at the Reformation Wall, Geneva, Switzerland

John Calvin, Hans Holbein the Younger (c. 1498–1543)

Postage stamp, circa 1964, of the influential French Reformer John Calvin

church insisted that all Vatican guards be Roman Catholics, as well as of sound ethical and moral background.

As one Swiss mercenary company went off to war, they took a chaplain with them: Huldrych Zwingli (1484–1531). Embedded with the army, Zwingli experienced the life of a soldier. He hated that Switzerland was sending the strongest of their young men off to fight foreign wars, which only weakened the Swiss's own defense. And he also opposed the commercial benefit from war.

Zwingli became known as the "People's Priest" in Zurich, where he would preach in the church on Sundays and in the town square on market day. His zeal, practices, and conviction earned him respect. His standing with the people caused the city council to legalize evangelical preaching and to end the practice of sending off mercenaries to foreign wars.

Sketch of Zwingli, published between 1905 and 1909, artist unknown

Though not as well known, Zwingli was a significant Reformer. He and Luther agreed on many doctoral points but disagreed strongly on the Lord's Supper. Zwingli's inability to agree with Luther slowed the progress of the Reformation tremendously, preventing the reformed states from taking a unified stand against the pope. This discord contributed to conflicts that resulted in religious wars. Zwingli eventually died in battle in 1531.

THE IMPACT OF JESUS ON THE RISE OF CAPITALISM

The reformation of the church occurred simultaneously with an economic rebirth in Europe. Although the economic boom existed independently of the changes in the church, the messages of the Reformers helped spur its continued growth.

The Protestant work ethic focused on personal gain, rather than gains for the lords or the church. It emphasized that work of any type could bring joy and religious significance. These new Reformers taught that a person's work can become his or her calling. As such, all people enjoyed equality in the eyes of God. They explained that God gave people work. *Secular* jobs could exalt God as much as religious vocations. In a real sense, all jobs were religious positions given by God to people. This message offered new dignity to workers and empowered them to excel.

The Reformers emphasized work ethic, encouraging the people to work diligently and honestly. As one's work was considered one's calling, a good work ethic brought glory to God in a person's everyday life. This shift in thinking helped give birth to capitalism.

John Calvin promoted another change that transformed business. Calvin taught that Christians could lend and borrow money, and that it was not usury for Christians to receive interest on loans. Until this time, the Catholic Church held that this practice was sinful. Calvin taught that as long as the interest charged was fair and reasonable (and did not promote disunity), it was acceptable. This concept opened up new business avenues, making working capital available to entrepreneurs and allowing for faster amassing of wealth.

John Calvin taught Christians that the ability to earn money was a gift from God.

In the end, Reformers taught that the ability to earn money was a gift from God. This different paradigm fit well with a culture that would become a capitalist society.

THE IMPACT OF JESUS ON RELIGIOUS LIBERTY

The struggle for religious liberty remained a consistent theme during the Reformation years. Many of the Protestant Reformers felt that individuals should have the right to follow God as their conscience directed, in obedience to God and His Word. The only authority for doctrine became the Bible (as they interpreted it). The central Reformation principle of the "priesthood of all believers" empowered each person on many levels—including the individual reading and interpretation of the Bible.

In Reformation churches, Christ was the only head. No pope, king, or other human could claim ultimate leadership. The participation of Christian laity in church government reintroduced a concept neglected for a thousand years in the Western church.

On the surface, this climate allowed growing religious liberty and tolerance. Unfortunately, some leaders of newly formed churches and religious groups proved just as intolerant as the leaders of the Roman churches from which they tried to escape. While the Reformers required a measure of religious liberty and freedom of conscience for themselves, they often denied it to others and forced them to adhere to their beliefs.

The Influence of Monks on Capitalism

Monks developed some reliable business practices. While committed to a life of poverty, their efforts built systems of accounting, managed money, and developed the infrastructure of capitalism. As entrepreneurs, they often created income to support their order with additional profits going to the church.

One particular monk named Fra Luca Pacioli invented double-entry bookkeeping with the publishing of his book *Summa de Arithmetica, Geometria, Proportioni et Proportionalita* in 1494.

As before, doctrinal differences hindered the message of Jesus Christ. All too often, differences of opinion about scriptural interpretation distracted from believers' common faith in Christ Jesus.

Stained glass of Christ

Jesus had special concern for the poor. He ministered to them often, healed their diseases, and fed those who were hungry. Jesus cared for the needy so frequently that His disciples assumed He had sent Judas away during the Last Supper to give a gift to the needy (John 13:29).

Although church history records some significant efforts in caring for the poor, many chapters in church history show a disregard for Jesus' teaching in this area. During the Middle Ages, the church (and many members of the clergy) became wealthy at the expense of the poor. Cathedrals were adorned with artwork and gold, paid for by the backbreaking work of the peasants.

The Reformation did not put a stop to all greedy behavior of church leaders, but it provided some new episodes that caused the love and teaching of Christ to shine in the lives of the poor.

Around this time, John Knox (c. 1514–1572), a chaplain in the Church of England, served King Edward VI (1537–1553) as his personal chaplain. When Mary Tudor (1516–1558) ascended the throne, she reestablished Roman Catholicism. With England now under the control of Mary and the Roman Catholic Church, Knox fled to Geneva, where he met John Calvin.

> **Jesus' Impact: Caring for the Needy**
>
> And he directed the people to sit down on the grass. Taking the five loaves and the two fish and looking up to heaven, he gave thanks and broke the loaves. Then he gave them to the disciples, and the disciples gave them to the people. They all ate and were satisfied, and the disciples picked up twelve basketfuls of broken pieces that were left over. The number of those who ate was about five thousand men, besides women and children. (Matthew 14:19–21)

Calvin greatly influenced Knox, teaching him Reformed theology and Presbyterian polity (a system of church governance). Upon returning to Scotland, Knox led the Protestant Reformation in Scotland, influencing the Scottish Presbyterian Church. This in turn heavily impacted later Presbyterian Church development.

In January of 1559, the Beggars' Summons was posted on the door of every friary in Scotland. Although anonymous, this document is most often attributed to John Knox. It urged the friars to release the money they had been

Mary Tudor by Antonis Mor (c. 1519–1575)

hoarding and use it to improve the lives of the poor and lower class. (Historians believe that during this time, over half the wealth of Scotland was in the hands of the clergy, who grew wealthier by the day.)

Knox felt that providing for the poor and needy was the work of the church, as stated in James 1:27. At the same time, he also believed people should work for what they received.

As the Reformation grew, more cities converted to Protestantism. Those cities then took over the work of the Catholic Church in caring for the poor.

THE IMPACT OF JESUS ON MUSIC

Since the time Jesus sang hymns with His disciples (Matthew 26:30), the church has used music as an act of worship.

Throughout the Middle Ages, the Catholic Church produced large volumes of music in Europe. The Catholic Mass contained extensive music, especially for Masses that celebrated holidays, coronations, weddings, and other special events. This music had a complex structure, written in multiple parts for multiple voices or instruments.

Originally, the music of the medieval Mass was sung by a choir made entirely of clergy. It was sung in Latin, to match the rest of the Latin Mass. While the complex structure and Latin lyrics served the objectives of the church, they placed music outside the musical ability of common people.

Just as the Reformers wanted to convert the scriptures and church service into the language of the people, they also sought to empower the people to make music of their own. In order to make music accessible to the masses, the Reformers urged the simplification of musical forms and lyrics, translating it into the vernacular of the people.

As part of this effort, leaders of the Reformation encouraged the development of choral music using four-part harmony, a simple structure that allowed people to sing together more naturally. They shortened songs, added repetitive refrains, and wrote lyrics in everyday vernacular. Like other aspects of new church services, the music itself could teach the people about Jesus and His work for them. Singing and listening to the music in the church became a natural and engaging way for people to learn about Christ.

Christian and Muslim Playing Ouds Catinas de Santa Maria Castile, King Alfonso X (1221–1284)

Martin Luther translated existing music of the Catholic Church into the common vernacular. He believed that "God announces the Gospel through music."[10] He used music to help center the service on Christ.

Luther wanted hymns to focus on God. He also wanted to keep them simple so people could easily sing them. He avoided fancy vocabulary and complex musical backgrounds. While he commissioned others to compose, Luther also composed his own hymns. His most famous hymn, "A Mighty Fortress Is Our God," remains popular in churches today.

Panel of a choir from *Cantoria* in the Cathedral of Florence, Luca della Robbia (c. 1399–1482)

While not all the Reformers agreed on the form and function of music, they shared an appreciation for its value. They relied on the Psalms extensively because they believed that God Himself authored the lyrics.

THE IMPACT OF JESUS ON EQUALITY OF EDUCATION

While the work of the monks to educate the people played an integral part in bringing about the Reformation, it suffered from the instability of the Reformation. Education had largely become a social class issue, with the upper classes receiving education and the lower classes missing out. As the lower-class children worked, they had no time to attend school.

Education became vitally important to Martin Luther and other Reformers. Luther observed that people who had little to no education couldn't read the Bible for themselves. As he believed that personal Bible study was a central part of being able to understand and apply scripture to one's life, this greatly troubled Luther. He also found that few clergy knew enough to teach others. He wanted education for the masses, as free of distinction for sex or social class as the gospel message he preached.

Luther was not alone in his interest in education. Philipp Melanchthon (1497–1560) and Johannes Bugenhagen (1485–1558), both of whom worked with Luther in the Reformation, shared the vision for public schools. Melanchthon was able to convince the civic authorities in Wittenberg to start a public school program. Bugenhagen was so instrumental in the organization of these schools that he has been called the father of German public schools.

Likewise, John Calvin and John Knox pushed the cause of education. They saw value in common people being able to read in their own vernacular rather than having to learn Latin. Calvin stated that education existed "for the purpose of training citizens for civil and ecclesiastical leadership."[11]

Long before child labor laws, the expectation was that everyone worked to support the family. Therefore, one of the biggest obstacles to education was the fact that children worked during the week, mostly in factories. Robert Raikes (1735–1811), an Anglican layman and philanthropist, expanded on a growing trend to help solve this problem: Sunday school.

Philipp Melanchthon by Lucas Cranach the Elder (1472–1553)

Medieval clerks studying astronomy and geometry, from the *Alexander Romance* in Old French prose, France (early fifteenth century)

Woman from the Middle Ages teaching geometry to students who appear to be monks

Raikes lamented that children ran the streets on Sundays, often getting in trouble. He realized that today's wild child could quickly become tomorrow's criminal. As the parents worked hard to provide for their families, most adults could not train their children. Raikes's Sunday school aimed to get children off the streets, teach them valuable skills, and introduce them to the teachings of Jesus. While he didn't invent Sunday school, Raikes pushed the practice forward and made it a place to teach children to read. The textbook was the Bible, which allowed children to learn moral principles directly from God's Word.

There are many reasons for Raikes's success. For one, he owned a newspaper and used it to promote his schools. Another important factor was that he catered to the needs of the student, rather than holding the student to a standard that most couldn't meet. The schools did not require expensive school uniforms; they simply required students to show up with a clean face and combed hair.

Raikes's Sunday school lasted about seven hours. In the mornings, the children arrived at ten for a lesson in reading. They returned home for lunch before resuming class in the afternoon. During the afternoon they engaged in additional reading lessons, attended a church service, and studied catechism.

Raikes's model became popular and contributed to lowering city crime rates. The work transformed the lives of those children.

The view of the Reformers toward education can be well summed up by a quote from John Knox:

> Seeing that men are born ignorant of all godliness, it is necessary that your honors be most careful for the virtuous education and godly upbringing of the youth of this realm, if either ye now thirst for the advancement of Christ's glory or desire the continuance of Gospel benefits to the generation following. For as the youth must succeed us, so we ought to be careful that they have the knowledge and erudition to profit and comfort that which is most dear to us, namely, the Church of Christ.[12]

Statue of Robert Raikes, founder of Sunday schools in the eighteenth century, London

QUESTIONS

1. How did Gutenberg's invention help set the Protestant Reformation in motion?

2. What challenges did Christian scholars face with the widespread circulation of Bibles printed in the original languages?

3. How did the Protestant Reformation contribute to the increase in literacy, education, and economical success among Europeans?

4. In what ways did Martin Luther and the Roman Catholic Church significantly differ in their views about the teaching of scripture?

5. Protestant Reformers believed that "*secular* jobs could exalt God as much as religious vocations." How did this belief influence people's work ethic?

6. How did Reformers like John Calvin help to change the Christian view of business and entrepreneurship?

Chapter 6

THE IMPACT OF JESUS ON THE FOUNDING OF THE UNITED STATES
(1700–1800)

Before Jesus' crucifixion, He was brought up on charges before Pilate. In one of the most intriguing stories of the New Testament, Jesus refused to speak at His trial. Pilate knew that if Jesus would defend Himself, the governor could easily justify releasing Him—but Jesus refused. Exasperated, Pilate said, "Do you refuse to speak to me? Don't you realize I have power either to free you or to crucify you?" (John 19:10).

Ecce Homo, Antonio Ciseri (1821–1891)

Jesus' profound response reveals a principle that has shaped history: "You would have no power over me if it were not given to you from above" (John 19:11).

In Jesus' reply, He announced that God empowers human government. Throughout history, some leaders have held themselves up as gods or equal to a god. Jesus' statement makes it clear: Kings, governors, mayors—all earthly powers—receive their authority from God. As such, God's law supersedes earthly law. God's will trumps the king's will.

This principle, shouted by the Reformers, impacted the understanding of law as new governments were emerging.

THE IMPACT OF JESUS ON AMERICAN EDUCATION

Vintage desks from an old schoolhouse

Soon after the Reformation fires spread across Europe, new colonies formed in America that were heavily influenced by the Reformers' ideals. One of the areas in which the Reformers' influence took root was the education of American children.

The earliest form of education in America occurred in people's homes, as parents taught their children between harvest and the next spring's planting. Families would also gather together in the local church building, which would serve as a community school during the week. Since most parents were literate, many of them could serve as the community's teachers, as their work schedules permitted.

The education of children became a challenge, however, because many families needed to devote their entire daily life to survival. The struggle between survival and education led the Puritans to pass the first education law in 1642. It required responsible men to check in on parents in order to ensure they were educating their children. These men were

to take account from time to time of all parents and masters and of their children concerning their calling and employment of their children especially of their ability to read and understand the principles of religion and the capital laws of this country.[1]

"See that you do not despise one of these little ones. For I tell you that their angels in heaven always see the face of my Father in heaven." (Matthew 18:10)

Early education, infused with Christian principles, used the Bible as a primary textbook. The school law of 1647 in Massachusetts, propagated just five years after the Puritans passed their law, contained the following statement: "It being one chief project of that old deluder, Satan, to keep men from the knowledge of the Scriptures."[2] The residents of these new colonies saw education as a means of ensuring that people could read the words of Jesus for themselves and thereby avoid being misled by Satan.

Other textbooks revealed Christian perspective. *The New England Primer*, the first reading primer published in the American colonies, was first published around 1688 and used for two hundred years. This book included "The Lord's Prayer"; "Morning Prayer for a Child"; "The Sum of the Ten Commandments"; "A Dialogue between Christ, a Youth and the Devil"; and children's stories that taught Christian character and values.

A Puritan couple walking through snow. The man holds a gun while the woman carries a Bible. Published by George Henry Boughton in 1885.

As the colonies matured, the founding fathers recognized the need for citizens defined

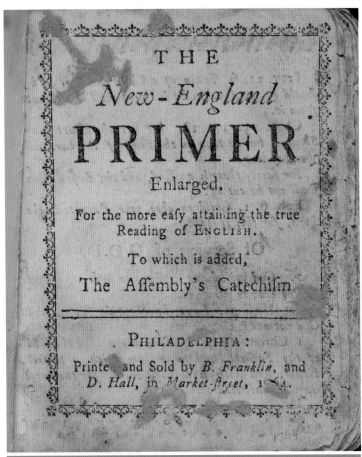

A 1764 version of *The New England Primer*, the first reading primer for American colonies, printed and sold by Benjamin Franklin

by their Christian worldview. They didn't separate their belief in Christ from their belief in a free country but rather used their belief in Christ to justify their belief in a free country. Benjamin Franklin is credited with saying, "A nation of well-informed men who have been taught to know and prize the rights which God has given them cannot be enslaved. It is in the region of ignorance that tyranny begins."[3]

The words of Samuel Adams (1722–1803) sum up the attitude of these early leaders:

Let divines and philosophers, statesmen and patriots, unite their endeavors to renovate the age, by impressing the minds of men with the importance of educating their little boys and girls, of inculcating in the minds of youth the fear and love of the Deity and universal philanthropy, and in subordination to these great principles, the love of their country; of instructing them in the art of self-government, without which they never can act a wise part in the government of societies, great or small; in short, of leading them in the study and practice of the exalted virtues of the Christian system.[4]

THE IMPACT OF JESUS ON THE SEPARATION OF CHURCH AND STATE

The Reformation changed the way the church and state operated together. In some cases, the Reformers became a common enemy that drew the church and state together. In other cases, the state was well served by the Reformers, and the state seized the opportunity to create a division between civil power and the church.

Although the Catholic Church had traditionally maintained a cozy relationship with the state, Reformers who opposed the teaching of the Catholic Church began to enjoy protections from the state. For example, Luther and Zwingli enjoyed protection by the state even though the Roman Catholic Church sought to punish them as heretics. And though some of these Reformers benefited from the protections of the state, the protection was conditional. They implicitly understood that the state provided protection as long as the Reformers served the purpose of the state. Luther even stated, "There is no way out, except through the arm of the government."[5]

> ### Jesus' Impact: God's Kingdom versus The World
>
> "Put your sword back in its place," Jesus said to him, "for all who draw the sword will die by the sword. Do you think I cannot call on my Father, and he will at once put at my disposal more than twelve legions of angels? But how then would the Scriptures be fulfilled that say it must happen in this way?" (Matthew 26:52–54)

In other cases, Reformers were persecuted by the civil government, just as they were by the official church of Rome. In these cases, turning one's back on the church to seek Christ was seen not only as heresy on the part of the church but as treason on the part of the government.

The Anabaptists (a radical group among the Reformers) strongly opposed the idea of the church and state working together. Menno Simons (1496–1561), the founder of the Mennonites, one of the principal groups of the Anabaptists,

SÉPARATION DE L'ÉGLISE ET DE L'ÉTAT

Caricature from *Le Rire* depicting the 1905 French law on the separation of church and state

grew angry at the relationship between the clergy and the state. In his mind, the clergy served the government rather than God. He spoke out against this relationship, stating that "no man or government has any authority against the Word of God."[6]

Anabaptists believed that the church of Rome had fallen so deeply into corruption that it needed replacement, not reformation. As a result, they totally rejected the idea of an intertwined church and government, as it had bred

The first Baptist church in America founded in 1638, Providence, Rhode Island

corruption and misinterpretation of scripture. Only a church completely free of the government could follow the teachings of Jesus.

Over a hundred years later, American Baptist churches, which held similar beliefs to the Anabaptists, strongly promoted the separation of church and state. Roger Williams (c. 1603–1683), founder of the first Baptist church in America, had experienced the corruption of the Church of England. As such, he advocated strongly for separation of church and state. The faith of many kings and queens waxed and waned with the winds of politics, which affected the monarchs' influence over the church and kept the church from remaining steadfast for Christ.

Even though the Separatists had traveled to America for religious freedom, Williams's general opposition to the king seemed too radical for many. The Massachusetts Bay Colony banished him. Williams sought a new beginning and founded the Providence Plantation (later named Rhode Island). Here he started the first Baptist church. Both the newly founded colony and Williams's church served as a sanctuary for those who experienced religious persecution. Anabaptists, Quakers, and Jews dominated the groups that settled in Rhode Island.

The first Europeans who set foot on North American soil intended to build a Christian community. Fleeing persecution in Europe, the Pilgrims (and later the Puritans) sailed for the Americas with the goal of obtaining religious freedom. They sought to worship God and Jesus Christ in the manner they chose without interference or mandates.

Before leaving Europe, William Brewster (c. 1567–1644), the leader of the Pilgrims, said he hoped the Pilgrims would advance the gospel of the kingdom. When they drew up the Mayflower Compact, the very first European political document in the New World, the Pilgrims began with the words "In the name of God, Amen." The compact also included the phrase "having undertaken for the glory of God and the advancement of the Christian faith." Regardless of what others who followed them may have thought, the Pilgrims saw themselves as forming a Christian colony.

The Mayflower Compact, 1620, Jean Leon Gerome Ferris (1863–1930)

Writing the Declaration of Independence, 1776, Jean Leon Gerome Ferris (1863–1930)

John Trumbull's (1756–1843) *Declaration of Independence* was used on the reverse side of the two-dollar bill.

As the colonies turned into states, many other Christian phrases appeared in founding documents. South Carolina, Connecticut, North Carolina, Delaware, Pennsylvania, New Jersey, Vermont, and Massachusetts all referred to God by a number of names: "one God," "Almighty," "Supreme Being," "the Creator," and "Great Legislator of the Universe."

The Declaration of Independence contains numerous phrases that reference God, even if they do not mention Him directly. The founding fathers believed that God extends rights to humanity. One central phrase has been passed down through the years: "that they are endowed by their Creator with certain unalienable rights, that among these are life, liberty and the pursuit of happiness."

> **Jesus' Impact:**
> **Freedom to Worship**
>
> "Yet a time is coming and has now come when the true worshipers will worship the Father in the Spirit and in truth, for they are the kind of worshipers the Father seeks. God is spirit, and his worshipers must worship in the Spirit and in truth." (John 4:23–24)

No matter where modern readers fall on the debate of whether today's United States should be considered a Christian nation, the Christian influence shaped the founding fathers' work. The original colonists enjoyed the freedom of religion and aimed to create a community where they could worship as they saw fit.

The desire to worship Jesus had a profound impact on the founding of the United States of America.

THE IMPACT OF JESUS ON HUMAN RIGHTS AND DEMOCRACY

As the North American colonies moved toward independence, the founding fathers of the United States struggled with the formation of a new form of government. Based on hundreds of years of experience with Europe's all-powerful leaders, they favored a government without a king, emperor, or other figurehead. They also recognized the problems of mixing powers of church and state, and determined to have a separation between the two.

Jesus' teachings strongly influenced the founding fathers, whose faith defined them. Those who might not have identified with the Christian faith were still heavily influenced by the prevailing Christian worldview. As such, they founded the new nation under biblical principles—chief among them was the freedom that Christ bestows to individual humans.

Men like Noah Webster (1758–1843) advocated that the new nation build on the foundation of the Christian religion. He believed people could rise above their own baser instincts and accomplish something for the common good only through devotion to God and adherence to the teaching of Jesus and the Bible. When humanity's actions neglected the precepts of the Bible, evil and corruption occurred.

John Quincy Adams (1767–1848), who became the sixth president of the United States, believed the Bible taught the concept of self-government. Along with others, he believed the law of human government could not over-ride the law of God.

Many of the founding fathers understood the responsibility they held in their hands. They knew the risks of opposing the English monarchy and began to see the form a new country might take. They believed that a government that honored the God-given value of its citizens must have a balance of power. The government needed to exist to consider the needs of all over the needs of a few.

Noah Webster, the "Father of American Scholarship and Education"

The framers of the United States Constitution placed their belief in God and the teaching of Jesus in the establishment of their new country. They set out to create a nation of laws and rights, firmly founded on scripture. Each citizen was to enjoy the rights endowed by the Creator.

John Quincy Adams, sixth president of the United States

THE IMPACT OF JESUS ON THE RULE OF LAW

Today historians herald the Magna Carta as one of the most influential political documents created. It affected the laws of England, influenced the US Constitution, and impacted the creation of governments around the world. The Magna Carta, however, had a rocky start in England.

Because King John signed the document under duress, he worked to undermine it. Later kings also despised it, as it limited their power. Finally, in the seventeenth century, Sir Edward Coke (1552–1634), at one time the attorney general of England, advocated the Magna Carta, declaring the king subject to the law.

Samuel Rutherford (c. 1600–1661), a Scottish Presbyterian minister, wrote *Lex, Rex*, a treatise on the importance of law. In it, he challenged the commonly accepted idea that the king and state ruled as God's agents here on earth. According to Rutherford, the Bible—and not a king—existed as the foundation for the law and all government. Put simply, he stated that the law of God trumped any human law.

The principles of *Lex, Rex* came directly out of the budding church movement formed during the Reformation. The new church explored the teaching of Jesus and the Bible deeply and embraced the differences Jesus spoke of between the kingdom of God and the kingdom of earth. God's throne supersedes humanity's kingdoms, and His Word trumps the edicts of earthly kings.

The English government burned *Lex, Rex* and made owning a copy punishable by death. The government also cited Rutherford for high treason. Nevertheless, *Lex, Rex* influenced the laws being written in America.

Another Scottish Presbyterian minister, John Witherspoon (1723–1794), studied *Lex, Rex* before setting sail for the New World. In addition to his role as a minister, Witherspoon became president of the College of New Jersey (now known as Princeton University) and a member of the Continental Congress. As part of the Continental Congress, Reverend Witherspoon was one of the signers of the Declaration of Independence.

The writers of the Constitution of the United States studied the Magna Carta, the English Bill of Rights, and *Lex, Rex*. While those documents dealt

The Sermon on the Mount, Carl Heinrich Bloch (1834–1890)

mostly with limiting the power of a king, many of the same freedoms they guaranteed were incorporated into the American Bill of Rights.

THE IMPACT OF JESUS ON SLAVE TRADE IN BRITAIN

Europe had mostly discontinued the practice of slavery by the fourteenth century, but the abominable practice resurfaced in the American colonies in the seventeenth century to provide labor for the large plantations in the South.

United States stamp (c. 1930) dedicated to the Magna Carta

Statue of John Witherspoon, Princeton, New Jersey (2005)

And though England had largely stopped the import of slaves for their own use, they voided their moral high ground by becoming heavily involved in shipping slaves from Africa to the American colonies.

William Wilberforce (1759–1833) emerged as a key British figure in the battle against the slave trade. Born to a wealthy merchant, William was a young man fully enmeshed in England's fashionable society. Running with the country's elites, he became friends with many important people, including William Pitt the Younger (1759–1806), who became prime minister of the British Empire in 1783.

An excellent and witty speaker, Wilberforce was elected to Parliament in 1780, at the age of twenty-one, and spent the next forty-five years of his life in office.

While in office, he was converted to evangelical Christianity and strove to follow Christ's teaching, which shaped much of Wilberforce's later work in Parliament.

Wilberforce promoted the importance of religion, morality, and education. While in Parliament, he championed many societies and causes that carried on a moral mission. He also supported many Christian works both at home and abroad. Some contemporary critics complained that he was too interested in helping people abroad and ignored injustices at home.

Wilberforce became friends with John Newton (1725–1807), a former captain of a slave ship who converted to Christ and became an Anglican priest. Newton gave Wilberforce an inside look at the workings of the slave trade. When Wilberforce was considering leaving Parliament to go into the ministry, Newton convinced him that he could serve God's purposes better where he was.

Slavery monument near a previous slave trade location in Stone Town, Zanzibar, Tanzania

Wilberforce's faith and his position in Parliament made him an important ally to the abolitionists, who convinced him that slavery was immoral and urged him to stand against the slave trade. Wilberforce became the abolitionists' voice in Parliament.

Witherspoon's Two Principles

Witherspoon touted two principles from *Lex, Rex* that ended up becoming part of the United States Constitution. The first of these was the principle of a covenant or constitution between the government and the people they ruled. Witherspoon espoused the idea that the government could not possess unlimited power without violating the law of God. The second principle was that God created all people equal. This fundamental viewpoint became a key statement in the Declaration of Independence, as a justification for not needing a king to rule.

The new nation would be bound by the rule of law, deferring to divine standards of ethics and justice. God's law superseded the power and authority of civil government. Officials did not possess absolute authority. This concept of the rule of law came directly from the writings of *Lex, Rex.*

It took twenty-six years, but Wilberforce finally succeeded in having the Slave Trade Act of 1807 approved by Parliament. The act forbade British ships from transporting newly acquired slaves, abolishing the slave trade anywhere within the British Empire. While this did not eliminate the slave trade, it greatly reduced it.

Wilberforce resigned from Parliament in 1825, but his voice still carried powerful weight. Later Wilberforce supported another campaign to abolish slavery in the British Empire. That campaign resulted in the Slavery Abolition Act of 1833. This law abolished slavery in the entire British Empire (with the exceptions of the territories in the possession of the East India Company and the islands of Ceylon and Saint Helena).

Three days after the passing of the Slavery Abolition Act, Wilberforce died. He had dedicated a large part of his life to setting people he never knew free, knowing that God had not created them to be slaves. While his efforts did not stop slavery in America, they helped create a culture that reduced the flow of slaves to the States and helped provide impetus to the abolitionist movement in the United States.

Replica of the United States Constitution

THE FRENCH AND AMERICAN REVOLUTIONS IN CONTRAST

The 1700s saw two major, successful revolutions in the Western world: the United States of America an France. Timing would make it seem like there should have been some similarity between these two revolutions, but they had little in common.

The American Revolution was a fight by people intent to throw off earthly tyranny and create a society in which God's rule underpinned humanity's law.

The French Revolution was fought by people looking to overthrow the king *and* the church. In France, like

Jesus' Impact: Serving Others

Jesus called them together and said, "You know that those who are regarded as rulers of the Gentiles lord it over them, and their high officials exercise authority over them. Not so with you. Instead, whoever wants to become great among you must be your servant, and whoever wants to be first must be slave of all. For even the Son of Man did not come to be served, but to serve, and to give his life as a ransom for many." (Mark 10:42–45)

most of Europe, the church was inseparable from the state. At times it was

A wood engraving of captives forced to walk in a coffle from the African interior, escorted by armed slavers from East Africa (1859)

impossible to tell where one ended and the other began. Each served the other.

To fight against the feudal government, the French people fought against the church. To transform their country, the French revolutionaries attacked the Christian faith as well. They sent anyone outside their camp to the guillotine.

The church's long history of perverting the teaching of Jesus and promoting religious wars in France produced an understandably agnostic outlook for the people. The church's oppressive nature earned their hatred. Eliminating the church became part of the larger battle of overthrowing the feudal system.

QUESTIONS

1. How did Christianity influence the education of children in the early American colonies?

2. Who were the Anabaptists, and how did they view the relationship between the church and government?

3. In what ways did the desire to worship Jesus and follow biblical truth directly affect decisions and legislation made by the Pilgrims, founding fathers, and early leaders of the United States?

4. How did *Lex, Rex* influence the formation of the Declaration of Independence and the Constitution of the United States?

5. How did William Wilberforce's faith in Christ motivate his work in the British Parliament? How did his efforts affect abolitionism in the United States?

6. What Christian beliefs were reflected by the ideals and objectives of the American Revolution?

Chapter 7

THE IMPACT OF JESUS ON THE AGE OF MISSIONS
(1800–1900)

G o and make disciples of all nations" (Matthew 28:19).

It is likely that no single command of Jesus has more motivated Christians throughout history. The church's efforts to follow this command and introduce the teaching of Jesus to people all over the world have changed the stories of individuals and story lines of entire countries.

In Europe, the Protestant church did not win the Reformation, but it survived and set itself up as a strong institution. Rather than overhaul the existing Catholic Church, Protestants began their own tradition, running in tandem with it. With their churches and viewpoint established, Protestants aligned their mission of making disciples of all nations with the age of expansion and exploration. Their mission field had two frontiers: (1) to take the gospel to people who had never heard it before and (2) to bring the message of reformation to areas of the world already evangelized by Catholic missionaries.

The Calling of the Apostles, Domenico Ghirlandaio (1449–1494)

One of the first Protestant missionaries to leave Europe, William Carey (1761–1834) traveled to Serampore, India (near Calcutta). Carey founded the Baptist Missionary Society and became known as the father of modern missions.

Carey traveled to India in 1793 with his wife, children, and his wife's sister. The church gave its blessing but not its financial support. Following the example of the apostle Paul, Carey supported his own missionary effort by working. He found a job managing a friend's indigo factory.

During his years working with the people of India, Carey learned the local language (Bengali). Within six years, he completed his first edition of the Bengali New Testament. Carey's appetite for Bible translation grew, and throughout his life he oversaw the translation of the New Testament into four

William Carey DD, professor of the Sanskrit, Marathi, and Bengali languages and missionary to India

languages and the Old Testament into two.

Carey exemplified a holistic approach to ministry. It wasn't enough to build churches and preach the gospel; he also sought to reform society. He built his plan for reformation on the foundation of scripture. He believed that while it was his duty to pray for

Jesus' Impact: Respect of Women

Jesus said to [the woman], "I am the resurrection and the life. The one who believes in me will live, even though they die; and whoever lives by believing in me will never die. Do you believe this?" (John 11:25–26)

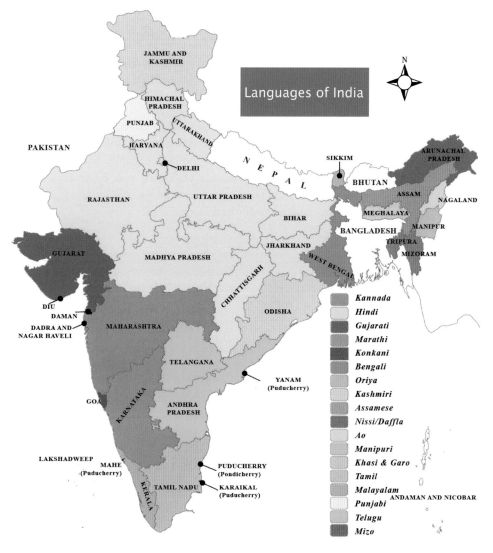

Languages of India

Kannada
Hindi
Gujarati
Marathi
Konkani
Bengali
Oriya
Kashmiri
Assamese
Nissi/Daffla
Ao
Manipuri
Khasi & Garo
Tamil
Malayalam
Punjabi
Telugu
Mizo

the salvation of people, only God could bring about their salvation and rescue them from their rebellion.

After six years, Carey left the factory and established a missionary school and community. He bought a large home where he housed and schooled missionaries.

Carey confronted more significant challenges than learning the language and creating a school. In India, he found a culture that did not share European values: a cruel caste system diametrically opposed to the teaching of Jesus to love your neighbor.

Carey evangelized the Hindu people and directly confronted the inequities he encountered in the Indian culture. He stood against social tiers and encouraged marriage between castes. He came to the defense of abused women by preaching against polygamy, female infanticide, child marriage, euthanasia, and forced illiteracy. Carey believed that women had purpose and rights that went beyond satisfying their husband's pleasure.

Carey also actively campaigned against *sati*, the practice of a recently widowed woman committing suicide at her husband's funeral. She would be urged or even forced to throw herself on his funeral pyre and burn to death. To Carey, this deplorable practice opposed the teachings of Christ, who considered all human life precious. Carey campaigned against the practice of *sati* for twenty-five years. The practice was finally outlawed in 1829.

WOMEN IN INDIA

Female missionaries in India took in thousands of abandoned children, saving their lives. Amy Carmichael (1867–1951), an Irish Protestant missionary to India, emerged as the greatest example of child protection in India at this time.

In 1901, Amy met a five-year-old girl who was being sold into slavery as a temple prostitute. The girl

A poor girl from India

resisted her family and temple priests and ran away. Amy took her in, provided her with shelter, and protected her from those who attempted to reclaim her. Withstanding considerable pressure, Carmichael refused to return the girl to the temple or her parents (who desired to restore the child to the temple).

The girl told Carmichael of the abuse and perversions of temple prostitutes. Amy's further research confirmed that this fate not only awaited young girls but many young widows as well. While these young widows had been saved from *sati*, many lived as prostitutes in order to survive in a society that did not care for widows.

Moved with compassion for these women and girls, Carmichael founded the Dohnavur Fellowship and rescued thousands from forced prostitution. To the children, she became known as "Amma," but the temple priests considered her a plague on their system. Temple officials charged her with kidnapping the children who fled to her and urged her arrest and imprisonment. Amy was charged with a criminal case, but never actually served her time.

The Dohnavur Fellowship grew through the years, expanding to rescue boys as well as girls. They also operated schools, hospitals, and printing organizations.

Amy spent her life battling the institution of temple

Amy Carmichael, missionary to India, with her treasured children

prostitution. Toward the end of her life, she won. In 1948, the Indian government outlawed temple prostitution, which moved the practice out of the temple. Today religious prostitution still widely exists, but the women work out of their homes or brothels.

WIDOWS AND ORPHANS

An Indian woman named Ramabai (1858–1922) joined the fight to end temple prostitution. Against established tradition, Ramabai's father had educated his child bride—a crime that earned him banishment from the city. From this marriage, Ramabai was born. Her father and mother continued to teach her until their deaths. Upon her conversion to Christ, Ramabai dedicated herself to the plight of girls and women in her country.

Ramabai built a center for widows in Pune, India. Within a few years, she had two thousand girls living in that center and hearing about Jesus. Ramabai led prayer meetings, preached, and held revivals. She cared for these girls until her death in 1922. The mission to widows in Pune is active today.

> **Jesus' Impact:**
> **The Preciousness of Children**
>
> "Then the righteous will answer him, 'Lord, when did we see you hungry and feed you, or thirsty and give you something to drink? When did we see you a stranger and invite you in, or needing clothes and clothe you? When did we see you sick or in prison and go to visit you?' The King will reply, 'Truly I tell you, whatever you did for one of the least of these brothers and sisters of mine, you did for me.'" (Matthew 25:37–40)

Earlier Catholic efforts of exploration and evangelism focused on the Far East and the Americas. Explorers established colonies, increased the wealth of their homelands, and extended the church's reach around the world. While the European Catholic missionaries were active in remote locations of the world, they neglected a closer neighbor: Africa.

As the Protestants established themselves in Europe, they launched new missionary efforts. Some worked to bring the Protestant message to parts of the world that the Catholic explorers had visited, and others embraced

Scottish missionary and explorer to Africa, Dr. David Livingstone (c. 1850s)

the African frontier. Like the Catholic missionaries who had gone to other colonies years earlier, this exploration combined dual goals of building trade and bringing the teaching of Jesus to those who had never heard it.

Africa contained new challenges for European missionaries. The land was vast and full of natural resources, but unusual culture stymied Westerners. The people seemed uncivilized. Life was harsh and the conditions dangerous for outsiders.

Many Christian missionary organizations worked alongside Europe's explorers to reach the indigenous people. Through these excursions, they sought to bring the gospel, industrialization, modern economy, and democracy to the people.

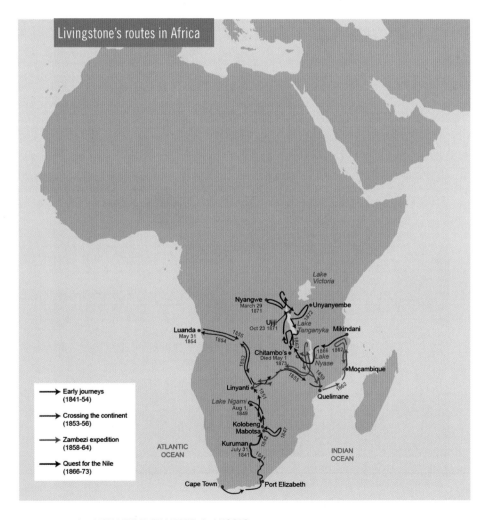

Livingstone's routes in Africa

Missionaries traveling to Africa in the nineteenth and twentieth centuries knew their life expectancy could be short. Disease, lack of medical care, strenuous travel, and the threat of martyrdom were real hazards of the work. This generation of missionaries saw themselves as following in Christ's footsteps and living out His example. They were willing to give their lives so that others might hear of Jesus.

Dr. David Livingstone (1813–1873) became one of the most well-known missionaries of this era. After training as a medical doctor, he traveled to Africa as both explorer and missionary. He mapped uncharted regions of the land and became the first known white man to cross the African continent.

Livingstone had a threefold goal: Christianity, commerce, and civilization. To achieve this, he traveled the continent, passing back and forth and mapping his finds. He developed friendly relationships with many tribal chieftains and cut covenants with over fifty of them. It was said that scars from these cutting covenant ceremonies covered his forearm.

Dr. Livingstone's Disappearance

In the late 1800s, Dr. Livingstone's reports back to England suddenly stopped, and the world lost track of Africa's missionary and explorer. After five years, a newspaper sent journalist Henry Morton Stanley (1841–1904) to find the doctor. It took another year and a half, and cost the lives of many of his party, but Stanley found Livingstone and supposedly uttered the now famous line "Dr. Livingstone, I presume?"

Stanley remained with Livingstone, continuing the work of exploring Africa with him. The two became good friends, but Stanley could not convince Livingstone to return to England with him. Livingstone died in Africa while kneeling in prayer next to his bed.

As a scientist, Livingstone also took great interest in the flora, fauna, and people of Africa. His observations and writings provided information about malaria, scurvy, and tropical ulcers. His extensive study of malaria led him to be among the first to determine the correct dosages of quinine to combat the disease.

Livingstone occasionally returned to the London Missionary Society and sent reports that found their way into British newspapers. His stories inspired many others to follow in his footsteps as missionaries to Africa despite the personal risks. Livingstone hoped that the maps he created, the notes he took, and the lessons he learned would help future missionaries bring the gospel to the African people.

MR. STANLEY,

IN THE DRESS HE WORE WHEN HE MET LIVINGSTONE IN AFRICA.

Stereoscopic Co.   Copyright.

Journalist Henry Stanley, a newspaper reporter hired by the *New York Herald* to find Livingstone

Livingstone inspired countless missionaries to serve in Africa, including Mary Slessor (1848–1915). She arrived at a missions compound in Nigeria that aimed to protect children and women. As she got to know the culture, she found one local practice particularly repulsive: the abandoning of twin babies. The natives believed twins to be the result of an evil spirit. They reasoned that one baby had natural origins and that an evil spirit had fathered the other. Because the natives could not distinguish between the naturally born baby and the cursed child, they would abandon both. Slessor began an orphanage and

Alexander Murdoch Mackay

rescued every abandoned baby she could find. Like Amy Carmichael in India, Mary found value in every life.

Slessor attained a mastery of the tribal language and gained the respect of the local villagers. She used her opportunity to preach the gospel of Jesus Christ to the people of Nigeria.

Alexander Murdoch Mackay (1849–1890), also inspired to the mission field by the work of Livingstone, traveled to Uganda. He shared Christ, and at the request of a tribal king, he taught farming, carpentry, and other manual skills to people in Ugandan communities. The people honored him with the name *Muzunguwa Kazi* (White Man of Work).

THE IMPACT OF JESUS ON THE BLIND

When Jesus walked the earth, He paid particular attention to people with disabilities and healed many. Specifically, the Gospels record stories of nine different blind people restored by Jesus. Each of them was unique, and Jesus treated them all with compassion, meeting their particular needs. This central compassion and love for others has become a hallmark of those who represent His teaching and strive to bring it to the world.

In 1809, a boy was born to a Christian family in France. At the age of three, the child grabbed one of his father's knives and tried to cut a piece of leather with it, as he'd seen his father do. Slipping, he pierced his eye, instantly blinding himself in one eye. Soon after an infection set in, he lost sight to his other eye. The child, Louis Braille (1809–1852), became permanently blind.

A local Catholic priest recognized Louis's intelligence. With the help of the priest, Braille won a scholarship to France's Royal Institute for Blind Youth. He excelled academically and musically, learning to play the cello, piano, and organ.

The school Braille attended owned few books that blind students could read. Each of these books used the Huey system, with embossed Roman lettering. Because of the size of the embossed print and the paper required to make the books, each volume was heavy and time consuming to read. Moreover, Huey's system offered some books to the blind, but it did not help the blind to write.

A visit from an army officer became a life-changing event for young Louis. Captain Charles Barbier developed a code called *écriture nocturne* (night writing) that allowed soldiers to communicate quickly and quietly in darkness. This system of raised dots and dashes fascinated Braille, and he learned it

Healing of the Blind Man, Carl Heinrich Bloch (1834–1890)

quickly. He offered ways to improve it, but Barbier rebuffed the criticism of a blind youth.

Using Barbier's system as a starting point, Braille developed a simpler system. Whereas Barbier had used columns of ten dots, as well as dashes, Braille used six dots and no dashes. The placement and arrangement of his raised dots allowed blind readers to quickly recognize letters.

By age fifteen, Braille had completed his system. Although he continued to work on it, adding music notation and other symbols, the original system that Braille created in 1824 essentially remains unchanged today. The first Braille book was published in 1829.

Louis Braille eventually became a teacher at the same school he had attended. He also developed a second system, Decapoint, which allowed blind writers to create embossed letters that could be read by sighted readers. When Pierre Foucault saw this

Jesus' Impact: Concern for the Blind

As he went along, he saw a man blind from birth. His disciples asked him, "Rabbi, who sinned, this man or his parents, that he was born blind?" "Neither this man nor his parents sinned," said Jesus, "but this happened so that the works of God might be displayed in him. As long as it is day, we must do the works of him who sent me. Night is coming, when no one can work. While I am in the world, I am the light of the world." After saying this, he spit on the ground, made some mud with the saliva, and put it on the man's eyes. "Go," he told him, "wash in the Pool of Siloam" (this word means "Sent"). So the man went and washed, and came home seeing. (John 9:1–7)

The Braille system of raised dots enables the blind to read.

Bust of Louis Braille

system, he developed the raphigraph, which allowed blind writers to punch dot letters that could be read by traditional readers.

Faith and Christianity directly affected and changed Braille's life, which has changed the lives of many blind people since. The Catholic church where Braille served as organist remained central in his life. Braille's faith is reflected in his last recorded words: "God was pleased to hold before my eyes the dazzling splendors of eternal hope. After that, doesn't it seem that nothing more could keep me bound to the earth?"[1]

The first Braille Bible was published in 1924.

When Jesus described the great white throne judgment, He said to those on His right, "Truly I tell you, whatever you did for one of the least of these brothers and sisters of mine, you did for me" (Matthew 25:40). Many categories of people could be called "least of these"—one is most certainly children.

The church has taken a strong interest in children from the day Jesus uttered, "Let the little children come to me, and do not hinder them, for the kingdom of heaven belongs to such as these" (Matthew 19:14).

THE FIRST ORPHAN HOUSES OPENED IN WILSON STREET APRIL 11th 1836

Original orphan houses known as Müller Homes on Wilson Street in Bristol, England

This legacy of the church continued in Europe through George Müller (1805–1898). The founder of orphanages and champion of children, Müller himself had been a troubled youth. Born into a middle-class family in Prussia, he was often in trouble. By the age of ten, he was known to be a liar, gambler, and thief; he even stole government money collected by his father. Müller's father sent him to college, hoping that a Christian education would reform the youth. Instead, Müller remained belligerent and drank heavily.

His life changed when a fellow student invited him to a prayer meeting, where those who gathered welcomed him. Müller began studying the Bible and discussing Christianity with others who attended the meetings. The moment of Müller's conversion came when he observed a man praying on his knees. The man's act convinced Müller that God was real and that He could be known. Müller's life changed immediately as he prayed for forgiveness of his sins and changed his ways. He renounced his previous habits of drinking, stealing, and lying and pledged to become a missionary.

Although Müller's father had wanted to see changes, he disapproved of his son's newfound passion to become a missionary. His father cut off his financial support in hopes of bringing his son to his senses. With tuition due, Müller prayed. An hour later, one of Müller's professors offered

Müller's Faith in God for Provision

Throughout his work, Müller refused to ask others for money. When he had financial needs, he asked God for what he needed and trusted in Him through faith. There are many anecdotes about Müller praying in faith for the needs of the orphanages. Below are a few of the better-known accounts.

One time the orphanage was out of milk and did not have money to buy more. Müller told the children to wait and boldly thanked God for the milk that He would provide. Shortly after Müller led the orphans in this prayer, a man knocked at the orphanage door. Outside they found a milk cart driver whose vehicle had broken down in front of the orphanage. The driver offered to share his milk with the orphanage.

On another occasion, a boiler in one of the orphanage buildings stopped working. Müller was concerned the children would suffer in the cold, so he prayed that the workers would work nonstop until the job was completed. He also prayed that the weather would improve until they completed repairs. Just before the workers arrived, a southern wind blew in and overcame the cold weather. And when the foreman arrived to end the workers' shift, the workmen requested permission to work through the night until the job was completed.

Old aluminum milk containers

him a position as a paid tutor, providing the needed income for Müller to continue in school. Müller discovered the power of prayer and faith and spent the rest of his life trusting God to provide for his physical needs.

While still in his twenties, Müller founded the Scriptural Knowledge Institute for Home and Abroad. He dedicated the institute to many causes,

Müller's Prayer Life

Rather than receive a salary, Müller prayed and depended on God for his physical needs. Whatever the need, Müller's answer was always to pray. He wanted to demonstrate to others that God remains trustworthy with the practical affairs of life.

including missions, Christian education, and the care of children. Over ten thousand orphans received care in the five orphanages Müller built in his lifetime. As a Christian organization, the Scriptural Knowledge Institute not only provided care for children but also ensured that each child received a faith-based education.

Although Britain outlawed slave trade in 1807, the owning of slaves wasn't made illegal until 1833. Even then, slavery flourished in other parts of the world, especially America, the Caribbean Islands, and Central America. In all these cases, slaves worked on vast plantations, fueling primarily agricultural economies.

The British Navy actively sought out and stopped ships involved in the slave trade. From 1807 to 1866, the Brits captured more than five hundred slave ships. Even with this effort, the slave trade proved too profitable, and the practice continued. While the British outlawed the use of their

Sailor walking among African captives in the hold of the ship. *Revelation of a Slave Smuggler* (1860)

Wood engraving (1860) of the slave deck of the ship *Wildfire*, which transported 510 captives from Africa to the Caribbean

commercial ships for slave trade, ships from other countries quickly filled the void.

The slave trade particularly troubled many Christians. Two British missionaries, John Leighton Wilson (1809–1886) and Dr. David Livingstone, worked to expose the cruel plight of the African slave trade. Both of these men witnessed how West African tribes and Arab slave traders kidnapped people from the interior of Africa and marched them up to five hundred miles. Bound in chains and led across the landscape of Africa, the captives were then forced onto traders' ships. The captors killed slaves who fell or stopped for any reason. Livingstone frequently wrote about the slave trade, and many of his reports found their way into British newspapers.

Livingstone's accounts of these atrocities had a substantial impact, stirring the whole of the civilized world against the slave trade. He called one active slave trader "a monster brooding over Africa"[2] and said that anyone might find the slave routes through Africa by following the patterns of vultures and hyenas that ate those who fell dead on the route.

When the leaders of the British Navy grew tired of policing the seas and chasing slave traders, John Leighton Wilson published a pamphlet discussing the importance of the task. The publication reinvigorated Parliament to renew efforts to stop the slave trade.

The work of Livingstone and Wilson met resistance because of the lingering market for slaves in North America. The writings of Livingstone and Wilson eventually crossed the Atlantic. Their message—coupled with John Newton's message—fed the abolitionist movement in the northern states.

Livingstone, Wilson, and Newton preached that the practices of the slave trade contradicted the moral principles found in Jesus' teachings. Jesus had taught respect and value of all people, and later the apostle Paul urged slave owners to treat their slaves like brothers, not like property or cattle.

Because of the prevailing arguments against slavery, many Americans began founding abolitionist societies bent on putting an end to slavery. In 1808, the area known today as Sierra Leone became a British colony populated by freed slaves from around the world. Inspired by the work in Sierra Leone, the American Colonization Society—whose members included Henry Clay, Daniel Webster, and James Monroe—established Liberia as a home for freed slaves. While members of the American

Henry Clay. Original artist unknown.

Colonization Society helped twelve thousand former slaves return to Africa, they had mixed motives. On one level, they tried to right a wrong by returning freedmen to their home continent. On another, they were driven by racial tensions in the United States and hoped to alleviate the problem by removing blacks from American society. While many took the opportunity to return to Africa, the majority of freed slaves preferred to stay in the only country they had ever known.

John Brown (1800–1859) grew dissatisfied with the pacifist effort of these abolitionist organizations. Eager for quicker results, Brown organized deadly raids against slave owners in Kansas. To keep his cause sustainable, he organized a raid on the federal armory at Harpers Ferry. Although he believed he was fulfilling God's plan, his attack failed, his followers were scattered, and Brown himself was captured, tried, and hung for his crimes.

Brown's illegal work helped propel the slavery issue to the forefront of national debate. The South seceded from the Union a year later, and the American Civil War began. The end of the war ended the slave market in the United States.

THE IMPACT OF JESUS ON LITERACY IN AFRICA

As Christian missionaries opened up new areas of Africa, commercial speculators followed closely behind and looked for opportunities to exploit people and resources. Governments sought to protect their countries' investors, and the Europeans moved to Africa to manage their mines, plantations, and other businesses. Before long, Europe controlled much of Africa.

Since the time Philip witnessed the conversion of the Ethiopian eunuch (Acts 8), Christianity has existed to some extent in Africa. Until the nineteenth century, however, European involvement (and Christianity) was mostly limited to the northern coastal areas. Other than Dr. Livingstone, few missionaries ventured far into Africa's inland.

Even though the West forgot about parts of North Africa and Ethiopia, the Coptic Church, the Alexandrian Church, and the Ethiopian Church—all African churches—were instrumental in the formation of the New Testament Greek text as well as orthodox theology. Christianity in Africa clearly did not originate with (nor did it depend on) Europeans.

Just as in Europe and the Far East, education opened up entry points for the church in Africa. Christian missionaries taught people to read and promoted Bible reading. Literacy became an important part of colonization efforts and later served the people in their quest to gain freedom from European influence. Educated Africans found work in the offices of the Europeans and helped shape the ruling class when the Europeans pulled out of Africa.

The missionaries who served Africa were a mixed blessing. Some had the best interests of the people in mind and fought commercial interest or colonial government to obtain them. Others were swayed by financial interests or

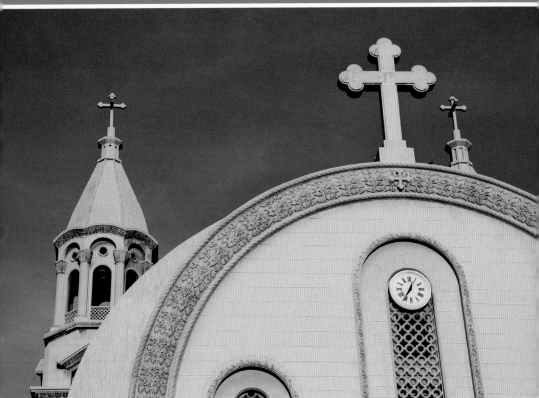

St. Mark's Coptic Cathedral in Alexandria, Egypt

intimidated by European powers and took advantage of the people they had once aimed to serve.

THE IMPACT OF JESUS ON RACIAL EQUALITY

In the United States, as well as in much of the rest of the world, misguided people have taught that one race is superior to others. Swedish professor Anders Retzius (1796–1860) propagated the idea that the races possess skulls of different size and shape, showing that they evolved from different species. Many people used ideas like this to promote that different races were unequal in their very nature.

In contrast, some Christians modeled the teachings of Christ and accepted all races as equal members of the human family, deserving of as much dignity and opportunity as any other. John Leighton Wilson debated racial evolutionary scientists who claimed that Africans were an inferior species. In his writings, he denounced the slave trade and supported the British Navy's effort to catch slave traders.

Portrait of Professor Anders Retzius, by Jean Haagen (1868–1938)

Many Christians saw the need for not only setting black slaves free but educating them as well. The education of all people, regardless of race, provided opportunity to better their lives.

Two institutions of higher education helped create avenues for education of African Americans during these formative years. The Presbyterian church founded Princeton Theological Seminary in 1812. The first black student to graduate from the seminary was Theodore Sedgwick Wright (c. 1797–1847) in 1828. Through his career, he was a pastor, abolitionist, and leader of the Underground Railroad. Many other influential blacks graduated from Princeton at a time when racial integration in educational institutions was highly unusual.

John Jay Shipherd (1802–1844) and Philo Penfield Stewart (1798–1868) founded Oberlin College in 1833. This Ohio college became the first college in the United States to enroll black students, which it did soon after its founding. Although most Christians associate Charles G. Finney (1792–1875) with his evangelism efforts during the Great Awakening movements, he also helped pioneer education efforts for women and blacks at Oberlin. Finney taught at Oberlin from the mid-1830s and became the school's president in 1851.

No Respecter of Persons

The Bible teaches that God created all humanity in His image (Genesis 1:26–27). While Jesus was born Jewish, He opened His heart and ministered to those who were not Jews, whether Roman, Greek, or Samaritan. Jesus actively demonstrated that the gospel message is for all humankind, regardless of race or ethnic background.

Billiard hall identified "for colored" on Beale Street, Memphis, Tennessee (1939), exemplifies Jim Crow laws

Although slaves obtained their freedom in the United States after the Civil War, improved opportunities for blacks would still not exist for African Americans in the United States. Christian organizations responded by founding many historically black colleges and universities to provide blacks with the possibility of higher education. These institutions provided the professional education necessary for African Americans to attain positions of importance and influence in society.

During the long, dark years where Jim Crow laws limited opportunities for blacks, these universities educated the doctors, lawyers, teachers, and ministers who built the black communities of the South. Eventually, educated members of these communities helped bring an end to Jim Crow laws and inspire Americans to live up to these words of Thomas Jefferson: "All men are created equal."

THE IMPACT OF JESUS ON THE POOR, HOMELESS, HUNGRY, AND DESTITUTE

The Industrial Revolution brought massive changes in society. Agriculture, which had traditionally depended on animal power and human workers, became mechanized. Many who had made up the agricultural work force explored new economic opportunities in the growing cities. At the same time, factory work became more mechanized, which created a need for fewer workers. The growing population and mechanization of factories left the cities with increasing numbers of jobless poor people.

Salvation Army volunteers sorting clothes (1942)

Many city residents could not find regular work and barely eked out a living. They often benefited from additional help to meet their most basic needs. New organizations offered a helping hand to these people—namely, the YMCA (Young Men's Christian Association), YWCA (Young Women's Christian Association), and the Salvation Army. Each of these organizations aimed to foster the spiritual growth and meet the physical needs of those struggling in city life.

William Booth (1829–1912) originally founded the Salvation Army in London in 1865. The purpose of the Salvation Army was to help the poor and introduce them to faith in Jesus Christ.

William Booth started his career as an evangelist in 1852. Rather than follow the traditional ministries of the church, he abandoned the pulpit and took the gospel to the streets, where he could speak directly to the poor and needy. Booth's unorthodox methods led to disagreement with church leaders in London, who insisted on more conservative methods of ministry. As a result, Booth stopped trying to work with the church and set out across England, preaching the gospel wherever he found people. After a series of meetings in the East End of London, Booth decided to remain there and minister to those in need.

Salvation Army volunteer collects money for charity

Booth's original goal was not to start a church but rather to convert people and then connect them to existing churches. At the time, this was a radical approach. Unfortunately, the churches weren't interested in the types of converts Booth was gaining and lacked the interest or ability to minister to them. Former prostitutes, drunkards, and gamblers did not fit in the refined atmosphere of the Church of England.

Since the church resisted these new converts, Booth trained them himself and sent them out to convert others. Within seven years, his Christian Mission grew from ten full-time workers to a group of one thousand, with forty-two evangelists.

Booth had never bothered giving his ministry a name, other than the "Christian Mission." He was the superintendent of the work, but his staff called him "the General." (The workers became commonly known as the Hallelujah Army.) The name *Salvation Army* became official when Booth was reading a printer's proof of the 1878 annual report. Seeing the statement "The Christian Mission is a volunteer army," he took up his pen, crossed out a few words, and wrote in the new name, "The Salvation Army."[3]

The Salvation Army came to America through Lieutenant Eliza Shirley (1863–1932). She moved to Philadelphia to join her immigrant parents and organized the Salvation Army's first US meeting in 1879. As the work grew, she sent a letter to General Booth requesting reinforcements, which she eventually received.

Jesus' Impact: Love and Equality

"But a Samaritan, as he traveled, came where the man was; and when he saw him, he took pity on him. He went to him and bandaged his wounds, pouring on oil and wine. Then he put the man on his own donkey, brought him to an inn and took care of him. The next day he took out two denarii and gave them to the innkeeper. 'Look after him,' he said, 'and when I return, I will reimburse you for any extra expense you may have.' Which of these three do you think was a neighbor to the man who fell into the hands of robbers?" The expert in the law replied, "The one who had mercy on him." Jesus told him, "Go and do likewise." (Luke 10:33–37)

Booth saw the need for the Salvation Army to develop a social relief system in order to help meet the needs of the people they ministered to. From its birth, the Salvation Army operated under the belief that charity would speed the work of evangelism by opening the people's hearts to hear the gospel message. Booth said:

> While women weep, as they do now, I'll fight;
> while little children go hungry, I'll fight;
> while men go to prison, in and out, in and out, as they do now, I'll
>   fight;
> while there is a drunkard left, while there is a poor lost girl upon
>   the streets, where there remains one dark soul without the light
>   of God, I'll fight!—
> I'll fight to the very end![4]

While the Salvation Army may have been the most successful of the organizations aiming to meet the needs of the poor and needy, it was not the only one.

The Red Cross and Jane Addams's (1860–1935) settlement house programs also helped those in need. As with the Salvation Army, these Christian organizations worked at meeting social needs and aimed to empower people to follow and serve God.

In some cases, the works of helping the poor, abolition, and women's suffrage blended together. Some workers, like Addams and Sojourner Truth (c. 1797–1883), a former slave, worked tirelessly to advance single mothers, women's suffrage, improved working conditions, a juvenile court system, and child labor laws.

Jane Addams (c. 1925)

THE IMPACT OF JESUS ON THE HUMANE TREATMENT OF PRISONERS

As cities and unemployment rates grew, so did crime. While professional criminals took advantage of city populations, many crimes were committed by poor people seeking to survive.

Prison conditions were horrible. Cells held thirty to forty prisoners in filthy, overcrowded conditions. Prison guards rarely let inmates outside their cells except to work at tedious and difficult labor. Prisoners who did not meet daily quotas were punished, and those in prison were expected to pay for their room, board, and services they received. (One of the services prisoners paid for was the unlocking of their shackles before being led into court.)

The mentally ill, petty thieves, and violent criminals lived together in the same prison cells. Physical abuse ran rampant, as did floggings and starvation. The facilities were unsanitary and had no heat. Women fared especially poorly and often had their children imprisoned along with them.

Wood engraving (1860s) of Elizabeth Gurney Fry reading to prisoners in Newgate Prison, London. Jerry Barrett (1824–1906).

The Quakers worked to apply Jesus' command to visit and care for those in prison. They became known for visiting prisons, bringing food and encouragement to those behind bars. They aimed to share Christ's love in hopes of reforming the lives of the criminals behind bars.

Quaker Elizabeth Fry (1780–1845) became one of the earliest prison reformers. Responding to encouragement from some friends, she visited Newgate Prison, just outside London. The conditions horrified her. She set to work immediately by bringing clothing and food to help the women and children imprisoned in Newgate. Fry eventually founded the Association for the Reformation of the Female Prisoners in Newgate, and her efforts grew into a nationwide organization.

It was slow work for Fry, with opposition from many sides. She opened a school in the prison to educate the children of the imprisoned women. She required women to sew and mandated that they read the Bible.

Jesus' Impact:
Love Your Enemies

"If you love those who love you, what credit is that to you? Even sinners love those who love them. And if you do good to those who are good to you, what credit is that to you? Even sinners do that. And if you lend to those from whom you expect repayment, what credit is that to you? Even sinners lend to sinners, expecting to be repaid in full. But love your enemies, do good to them, and lend to them without expecting to get anything back. Then your reward will be great, and you will be children of the Most High, because he is kind to the ungrateful and wicked." (Luke 6:32–35)

When her brother-in-law was elected to Parliament, he championed her efforts to reform Britain's prisons.

Elizabeth Fry succeeded in exposing the plight of prisoners—especially women. She became the first woman to present evidence before Parliament, testifying before a House of Commons committee in 1818. Her reputation and influence grew, and she gained a supporter in Queen Victoria, who granted her several audiences and provided financial assistance for her work.

Dorothea Dix (1802–1887) took up the cause for prisoners in the United States. She advocated for better conditions and special care for the mentally ill. She wrote reports of the terrible conditions and lobbied widely for prisoners in many states and at the federal level.

Dorothea Lynde Dix, US Library of Congress

The poverty that overcame cities severely struck children. Without labor laws or mandatory schooling, poor or orphaned children were forced to work while wealthy children enjoyed endless opportunities for school, leisure, and travel.

The plight of these children went ignored by many in society, but the church began to stand up for the rights of its youngest members. In 1881, Rev. George Staite wrote, "Whilst we have a Society for the Prevention of Cruelty to Animals, can we not do something to prevent cruelty to children?"[5] During that time, it was commonly believed that the government could not regulate what went on within a child's home. Legislation to improve the life of children seemed unrealistic.

Anthony Ashley Cooper, the 7th Earl of Shaftesbury (1801–1885), was raised by a very strict father until the age of eight, when his father died. He spent the rest of his

Anthony Ashley-Cooper, 7th Earl of Shaftesbury, John Collier (1850–1934)

youth in the care of custodians arranged by his father. His childhood left him with a sensitivity to seeing others suffer any form of cruelty. Even as a child, he decided to commit himself to doing something about the problems of the poor. At the age of twenty-five, he became a member of Parliament.

In 1884, Lord Shaftesbury, along with Rev. Benjamin Waugh, founded the National Society for the Prevention of Cruelty to Children. After five years of lobbying, Parliament enacted the first Prevention of Cruelty to Children Act of 1889. This act sought to protect children and to punish those who would abuse or neglect them. It also created restrictions for where and how long children could work. The Prevention of Cruelty to Children Act gave police permission to enter a home in the event they thought a child was in danger. It also outlawed the use of children for begging.

Shaftesbury's organization established the Ragged School Union for the education of destitute children. Unlike other schools, these schools provided food, free education, clothing, and lodging. Ragged schools' curriculum included the Bible, reading, writing, and arithmetic. In some of

Boy from West Virginia who worked in the coal mines (1908).

the schools, the curriculum expanded to include industrial and commercial subjects.

Lord Shaftesbury campaigned to outlaw children doing hazardous work. Climbing boys were used by chimney sweeps to climb on the roofs and clean out chimneys. With England's slate roofs, this was life-threatening work; many fell from roofs, especially on rainy days.

Foremen also sent children into coal mines. Queen Victoria (1819–1901) ordered an investigation after the deaths of twenty-six children in a flooded coal mine. Lord Shaftesbury led the inquiry and published the results in 1840. In his report, he appealed to Victorian sensibilities and to the society on behalf of girls who had worked in the mines and had consequently become unfit for marriage and motherhood. His report created quite a stir, helping the passage of the bill to outlaw the use of children in the mines.

While the National Society for the Prevention of Cruelty to Children was the first of its kind and the most active organization in working to alleviate the plight of children, groups like the YMCA also worked to help. In 1853, Rev. Charles Loring Brace (1826–1890) established the Children's Aid Society in New York, which offered services for poor, homeless, and disabled children as well as for struggling families.

Dust-covered breaker boys at a Pennsylvania coal mine (1911). Breaker boys used hammers to separate slate rock from mined coal.

QUESTIONS

1. How has missionary William Carey been compared to the apostle Paul in his approach to missions?

2. According to the reading, what made Amy Carmichael "the greatest example of child protection in India" in the early twentieth century?

3. In what ways did missionaries David Livingstone, Mary Slessor, and Alexander Mackay follow Christ's example of selflessness in their work in Africa?

4. How did George Müller show his unwavering trust in God's provision in his work with orphans?

5. How were European missionaries in Africa a "mixed blessing" for the African people?

6. Why was education viewed as important to Christians in the struggle for racial equality in the United States?

7. In what ways did the Salvation Army work to meet the social, physical, and spiritual needs of people in London and in the United States in the late nineteenth century?

Chapter 8

THE IMPACT OF JESUS ON THE MODERN AGE

(1900–Present)

G od promised His people, "Never will I leave you; never will I forsake you" (Hebrews 13:5). Yet when we look at our modern-day world, it is tempting to ask, Where is God? Does the church still have influence? Does the message of Christ still resonate with people? When culture promotes abortion and abandons the most sacred values of the Bible, does it mean Jesus and His teachings no longer have power or weight?

Nothing could be further from the truth. The work of the cross is as powerful in modern times as it ever has been. Even though the world is too distracted to look at Jesus, the impact of Jesus can be found.

The cross, the central image of Christianity

The world changed in 1927 when the first shortwave radio signals traveled from the Netherlands to Indonesia, a distance greater than 7,000 miles (11,000 km). Missionaries quickly grasped the importance of this change and by 1931 began using the radio to broadcast the teachings of Jesus Christ. For over eighty years, shortwave radio has been used to further the gospel message.

Shortwave radio frequencies differ from typical radio signals that have a range of only sixty miles. Shortwave transmitters can broadcast nearly one-third of the earth's circumference. With the aid of radio, missionaries can transmit the teaching of Jesus where churches cannot exist.

Jesus' Impact:
Transmission of the Gospel

"My prayer is not for them alone. I pray also for those who will believe in me through their message, that all of them may be one, Father, just as you are in me and I am in you. May they also be in us so that the world may believe that you have sent me. I have given them the glory that you gave me, that they may be one as we are one—I in them and you in me—so that they may be brought to complete unity. Then the world will know that you sent me and have loved them even as you have loved me." (John 17:20–23)

Use of radio has dramatically furthered the reach of the gospel.

With an estimated six hundred million shortwave radios worldwide, there are few places where one can go and not be able to hear the message of the cross over the airwaves.

Reach Beyond, a worldwide missionary organization, works with global partners to bring their radio ministry to the world. Wayne Pederson, president and CEO of Reach Beyond, says, "With all the technology, knowledge and experience available to us today, there is no reason why we can't make Christ known to everyone on the planet."[1]

The impact of shortwave radio was only recently passed by the worldwide embrace of the Internet. Today millions of faith-based web pages, blogs, and videos strengthen the faith of Christians around the world and provide opportunities for people in nearly every region of the world to hear the gospel.

THE IMPACT OF JESUS ON NEW DEAL AMERICA

The Great Depression changed the world beginning in 1929. While it began as an American event, its impact was felt worldwide.

Prior to the Great Depression, the United States was considered the land of opportunity, one in which everyone had the same chance for success. Hard work was the key to financial prosperity; those who worked could succeed.

Jesus' Impact:
Hope for the Indigent

"Peace I leave with you; my peace I give you. I do not give to you as the world gives. Do not let your hearts be troubled and do not be afraid." (John 14:27)

Row of unemployed men during the Great Depression, New York City docks
(c. 1930s)

Before this point, the American people often viewed public assistance as a crutch. Even those who could have benefited from it tried to avoid it, feeling a stigma attached to any aid received. Citizens and immigrants alike wanted to work and make their own way.

The Great Depression quickly changed perspectives. A desire for hard work wasn't enough if there was no work available. Many people who were willing to work—and wanted to work—couldn't find jobs. Charitable organizations could not keep up with the needs. In many cases, funds dried up for these relief groups. Without contributions, the church and parachurch organizations could not actively help the poor. The government stepped in to take the burden of providing social services off the back of the church.

While many conservative Christians hotly debate the benefits of social welfare, the social welfare services were instituted by leaders who believed the teachings of Christ and strove to improve their society. President Franklin

Roosevelt signs the Social Security Act (August 14, 1935). Among those standing behind Roosevelt are Secretary of Labor Frances Perkins.

Roosevelt (1882–1945) believed that the right course was to care for the hurting and that these services aligned with Jesus' urging to help the indigent.

Roosevelt believed that for the country to move forward, it was necessary that all parts of its citizenry flourish. Once people moved off the streets and had sufficient food, they would be able to focus on their spirituality. He believed that the social programs of the New Deal modeled Christ's compassion, and that if the government met the physical needs, the church could meet spiritual needs.

Roosevelt appointed Frances Perkins (c. 1882–1965) as the secretary of labor. She was the first woman ever to serve as a United States cabinet secretary and held the position for twelve years. Perkins's Christian convictions were at the base of Roosevelt's New Deal, which she helped create. The New Deal established the first minimum wage, social welfare, and Social Security. To Perkins, these acts of civic duty were acts of Christian love, charity, and responsibility.

In 1917, William Cameron Townsend (1896–1982) traveled to Guatemala with the hopes of selling Spanish Bibles in the area near Antigua. He quickly discovered that his Bibles did not have a market because the people in this area spoke Cakchiquel, not Spanish. When Townsend learned that the Bible did not exist yet in that language, he abandoned his sales career and began a new career as a linguist. He spent thirteen years capturing the Cakchiquel language in writing so that he could translate the Bible into their native tongue.

After this work, Townsend continued translating the Bible into other native languages, setting up linguistic training camps for language study and translation. Ultimately, this led to the foundation of Wycliffe Bible Translators, the best-known Bible translation organization in the world.

Missionaries around the world have replicated Townsend's model. With a desire to bring the written Bible to each people group, Wycliffe's missionaries immerse themselves in a new language and create a written alphabet for the native tongue. They teach the locals to read and translate the

Wycliffe Translation Efforts

Wycliffe expects their missionaries to invest many years with the people group for whom they will be translating the Bible. They must learn the language thoroughly and develop a written language for the people. Then they have to teach it to the people so that the community can read the forthcoming Bibles. Every Wycliffe translation effort takes an average of fifteen years.

Genesis 1 in Hausa. This language is spoken in Nigeria and Cameroon.

FARAWA

1 A chikin farko Allah ya halitta sama da ƙasa. 2 Ƙasa kwa sarari che, woñ kuma ; a kan fuskar zurfi kuma sai dufu : ruhun Allah kwa yana motsi a bisa ruwaye. 3 Kuma Allah ya che, Bari haske shi kasanche : haske kwa ya kasanche. 4 Allah kwa ya ga haske yana da kyau : kuma Allah ya raba tsakanin haske da dufu. 5 Allah ya che da haske Yini, dufu kwa ya che da shi Dare. Akwai maraiche akwai safiya kuma, kwana ɗaya ke nan. 6 Allah kuma ya che, Bari sarari shi kasanche a tsakanin ruwaye. shi

kin nan biyu ; babban domin shi yi mulkin yini, ƙaramin domin shi yi mulkin dare : ya yi tamrari kuma. 17 Allah kuma ya sanya su chikin sararin sama domin su bada haske a bisa duniya, 18 su yi mulkin yini da dare, su raba tsakanin haske da dufu kuma : Allah kwa ya ga yana da kyau. 19 Akwai maraiche akwai safiya kuma, kwana na fuɗu ke nan.

20 Kuma Allah ya che, Bari ruwaye su yawaita haifan masu-motsi wa ɗanda ke da rai, tsuntsaye kuma su tashi birbishin duniya chikin sararin

Bible so that each people group can become literate and read the teachings of Christ.

Wycliffe typically oversees about one thousand ongoing translation projects. The ministry publishes about thirty new translations of the Bible per year. While they are not the only organization doing this work, they are the largest. Additional help comes from the United Bible Societies, the Scripture Gift Mission, the Trinitarian Bible Society, and translators from the Roman Catholic Church.

THE IMPACT OF JESUS ON THE JEWISH PEOPLE

Germany was in financial shambles after World War I. The economy lay in ruin, and the people lived in poverty. These desperate times became a fertile breeding ground for Adolf Hitler (1889–1945) and his National Socialist Movement.

Although raised a Catholic, Hitler wouldn't permit the church to have the control that he desired for his own party. Hitler saw the church as competition for the state, drawing people's loyalty away when he wanted the German people to declare total loyalty to the state.

As the Nazi Party grew in power, many churches aligned themselves with it in order to survive. The Vatican signed a concordat with Hitler, which allowed them to operate freely in Germany. While the Vatican may have signed this in good faith, Hitler violated the treaty almost immediately. Hitler once said, "The heaviest blow that ever struck humanity was the coming of Christianity. Bolshevism is Christianity's illegitimate child. Both are inventions of the Jew." [2] Feeling pressure from the state, many churches adopted rules that prevented them from allowing any people of Jewish origin to work in the church in any capacity.

The original German caption of this photo of Jews from the Warsaw Ghetto read, "Forcibly pulled out of dug-outs" (1943).

Hitler's personal hatred of the Jews was manifest in his solution to kill all Jewish people found in German-controlled lands. While this was common knowledge in Germany, few spoke out against it. Even many churches remained silent about the Jewish persecution, not wishing to incur the government's wrath. With the government watching the churches carefully and increasing its control over them, many were not willing to suffer the fate of those who took a stand against the actions of the Nazi Party. Later many of these denominations issued formal and informal statements confessing their guilt in not helping the Jews in their plight.

Because of the corrupting influence of the Nazi Party, Dietrich Bonhoeffer (1906–1945) aimed to restore the true gospel to the German church. He became a founding voice of the Confessing Church, which rejected the state's totalitarian claims and interference in religious matters. Naturally, the government opposed the movement and began persecuting the Confessing Church. Many of the leaders joined the resistance movement against Hitler and their own government.

The German government banned Bonhoeffer from preaching openly. While he limited public speaking, he continued teaching in underground seminaries. Offered the opportunity to escape to the United States, he believed God's plan for him was to effect change in Germany. On the

Blessing the Jewish People

While many failed, some Christians did what they could to promote Christ's compassion and love. These people risked their lives to save fellow citizens of Jewish descent. One of the best-known underground leaders involved in helping the Jews was Corrie ten Boom (1892–1983). Born in Amsterdam, she grew up in a devout Christian family. They sheltered Jews in their home and worked as an underground hub, moving Jews out to rural areas of Holland, where they could find safety.

Eventually, the Nazis discovered the efforts of the Ten Boom family and sent them to the same concentration camps that housed the Jews. Only Corrie survived. Together with her sister Betsie, Corrie cared for the women imprisoned with her and read to them from a compact Bible she had managed to hide. Corrie's father, Casper, died after only ten days in prison, at the age of eighty-seven. He courageously faced his death, faithfully living out the statement he once shared with Corrie: "It would be an honor to give my life for God's ancient people."[3]

German Lutheran pastor and theologian Dietrich Bonhoeffer, founder of the Confessing Church (1939)

temptation to travel and stay in America, he said, "I must live through this difficult period in our national history with the Christian people of Germany. I will have no right to participate in the reconstruction of Christian life in Germany after the war, if I do not share in the trials of this time with my people."[5]

Returning to Germany, Bonhoeffer served as a double agent in hopes of weakening Nazi Germany and strengthening the church. He used his contacts at churches across the country to help Jews escape from the Nazis. Although he hoped that the Jews would convert to Christianity, he also believed that regardless of their religion, victims of injustice must be assisted.

Bonhoeffer's reward for helping Jews escape was his arrest in 1943. He was tried and executed on April 8, 1945. Hitler died less than one month later, and the camp was liberated.

CHRISTIAN INVOLVEMENT IN THE ESTABLISHMENT OF THE MODERN NATION OF ISRAEL

Few are aware of the role Christians played in the rebirth of Israel. William Hechler (1845–1931), a pastor and chaplain to the British Embassy in

Vienna, was consumed with the goal of Jewish restoration to Israel. Hechler heavily influenced a man named Theodor Herzl (1860–1904), a Jewish-Austrian journalist and political activist who promoted Jewish immigration to Israel. Herzl became known as the founder of the Zionist movement.

Lord Shaftesbury was also passionate about a Jewish homeland. He successfully prompted England to develop a policy in favor of returning the Jews to Israel. The Church of Scotland sent Andrew Bonar (1810–1892) and Robert Murray M'Cheyne (1813–1843) to investigate the circumstances of the Jews. Their findings were promoted in Britain followed by a "Memorandum to Protestant Monarchs of Europe for the restoration of the Jews to Palestine," which was "printed verbatim in the *London Times*, including an advertisement by Lord Shaftesbury igniting an enthusiastic campaign by the Times for restoration of the Jews." [6]

Other Christians campaigned for the cause, including Arthur James Balfour (1848–1930), who believed he was carrying out God's work to lobby for a reborn state of Israel. Balfour was joined in his efforts by his longtime friend David Lloyd George (1864–1945). George became British prime minister and offered a public platform for the effort.

In 1948, the United Nations voted to deed part of the British-controlled region of Palestine to the Jews. In hopes of creating peace for the Jewish people who had suffered in World War II, the United Nations drew boundaries between the new Jewish areas and the Arab people already living in the area. On May 14, 1948, the nation of Israel was reborn.

The Arab countries responded to the declaration by attacking the newly born nation. David Ben-Gurion (1886–1973) became the first prime minister of Israel and led the country through years of ensuing wars.

Former prime minister of the United Kingdom, David Lloyd George (1919)

In many cases, the Jews who returned to Israel fled persecution where they were living. Six million of them had already been killed by the Nazis. After the war and before the United Nations' declaration creating the Jewish homeland, Jews in Arab countries were persecuted and harassed. Even the Jews who lived in the lands of the old Soviet Union suffered.

Helping these people resettle their historic land seemed benevolent to many. Building Israel into a nation was difficult, but the chance for freedom gave the Jews the motivation to suffer the journey and work to create their homeland.

From the beginning, Christian organizations worked to help Jews return to their homeland. Christians have had different motivations for helping Jews return to Israel, and these still cause Christians to support the nation of Israel today. The faith-inspired reasons include (but are not limited to) the following:

- The belief that the Jews' return to Israel is prophecy being fulfilled.
- The belief that supports Christian Zionism, which mixes politics and religion. Those who promote this viewpoint hold that God continues His ongoing faithfulness to the chosen people of Israel.
- The belief that the Bible teaches us to maintain support for the Hebrews.
- The belief that Christians must demonstrate Christ's love to oppressed people. The pain of the Holocaust and the anti-Semitism demonstrated around the world requires that we treat the Hebrew people with love.

THE IMPACT OF JESUS ON CARING FOR THOSE IN NEED

The writer of the book of James echoed Jesus' passion for the poor, saying, "Religion that God our Father accepts as pure and faultless is this: to look after orphans and widows in their distress" (James 1:27).

Efforts to help the poor and needy of the world greatly intensified in the twentieth century. The advent of television and radio made it possible for Christian charitable organizations to reach many and recruit broad support for large causes.

One of the biggest of these modern-day charities remains World Vision. Originally founded in 1950, World Vision aims to increase awareness about hungry and poor people. Within a few years of their founding, they pioneered the system of individual sponsorship used to help the impoverished around the world.

World Vision now works in nearly one hundred countries providing child protection, disaster relief, economic development, education, food, refugee aid, health care, and agriculture.

Many Christian institutions desire to combat poverty. These include Food for the Hungry, Samaritan's Purse, Feed My Starving Children, and many others. While they hope to relieve the suffering of the poor, they

Compassion International

Compassion International is another sponsor-based Christian organization specializing in helping the poor and needy. Founded by Reverend Everett Swanson in 1952, Compassion International's initial purpose was to provide food, shelter, education, health care, and Christ's message to Korean War orphans. The organization now serves over twenty-five countries, focusing on children living in poverty.

Children in India

each look for creative ways to bring a broad range of services to those in these impoverished countries.

Because government bureaucracies move slowly to provide disaster relief, the church and parachurch organizations have designed quick response teams that bring relief after a natural disaster.

Christian agencies like Samaritan's Purse provide rapid emergency assistance through the relationships they already have with churches in the area. By providing instant infrastructure and relief, Samaritan's Purse helps local churches become the centers of help. Samaritan's Purse provides emergency relief through meeting the people's daily needs—giving them blankets, food, personal hygiene supplies, and cooking utensils. They build medical facilities and provide medicine and other essential supplies to people who have suffered through a natural disaster. They also provide emergency shelters for those who have lost their homes.

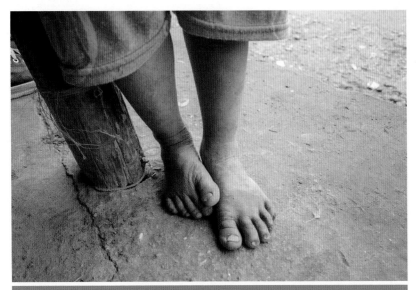
A child from Laos

THE IMPACT OF JESUS ON LEPER COLONIES IN INDIA

During the colonization period of history, leprosy was dealt with poorly. Because leprosy was not common in Europe, colonial government officials were poorly equipped to deal with lepers. People feared those with this disease and didn't know how to treat the illness.

In 1873, scientists discovered the bacterium that causes leprosy. This revelation drastically altered the way caregivers could treat this dreadful affliction. Recognizing it as a contagious disease, the British feared it would spread from India to England.

Although the government took an interest in helping lepers, it was the work of missionary organizations that made the biggest strides in fighting the disease and caring for its victims. In the nineteenth and twentieth centuries, missionaries took on the responsibility of caring for lepers. The Mission to Lepers, founded by Wellesley Bailey (1846–1937), believed it was the biblical responsibility of Christians to minister to people with the disease. While these missionaries ministered to the needs of lepers in many ways, their biggest campaign was to show them compassion.

Other ministries and agencies joined the work as well. Most felt that the greatest need that lepers had was to hear the gospel message and be given

Humanitarian aid from the Franciscan friars in tanzania, Africa

the chance to accept Jesus Christ as their Savior. By 1910, there were thousands of missionaries from more than thirty countries in India—many serving lepers.

During the early twentieth century, a surgeon named Paul Brand (1914–2003) moved to Vellore, India, to work and teach at the Christian Medical College and Hospital. A second-generation missionary, Brand pioneered developing surgical techniques for the restoration of deformities to lepers' hands and feet. He was also at the forefront of teaching those afflicted by leprosy how to better their lives by managing the disease and caring for themselves.

Jesus' Impact: Caring for Lepers

A man with leprosy came to him and begged him on his knees, "If you are willing, you can make me clean." Jesus was indignant. He reached out his hand and touched the man. "I am willing," he said. "Be clean!" Immediately the leprosy left him and he was cleansed. (Mark 1:40–42)

Of all the missionaries to India, Mother Teresa (1910–1997) received the most publicity in recent times. Her ministry focus was the poor of Calcutta,

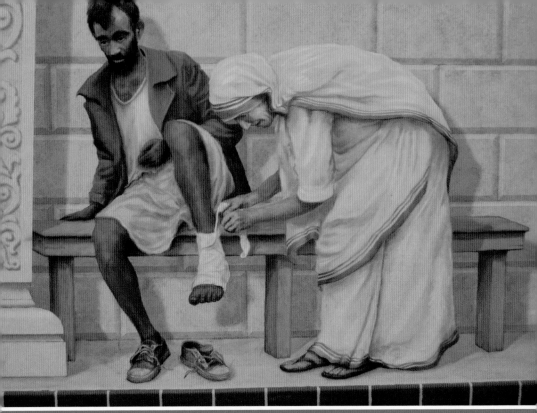

Fresco of Mother Teresa, Cathedral of Saint Augustine in Tucson, Arizona

where she frequently encountered lepers. In 1979, she earned the Nobel Peace Prize for her work. Upon accepting it, she said that she was receiving the prize "in the name of the hungry, of the naked, of the homeless, of the blind, of the lepers, of all those who feel unwanted, unloved, uncared for throughout society. . . . Though I'm personally unworthy, I'm grateful and I'm very happy to receive it."[7]

THE IMPACT OF JESUS ON EQUALITY IN AMERICA

When slavery ended in the United States in 1865, black Americans received their freedom, but they did not receive equal rights. Racial segregation and discrimination were rife. The official "separate but equal" policy did not even achieve similar facilities; it certainly did not provide an atmosphere of unity among all people.

The American civil rights movement was largely a Christian movement. While not all Christians agreed on the equality of blacks, enough became involved to encourage sweeping social reform.

Some major denominations took a bold stand in support of racial equality. The Presbyterian Church of the United States issued statements supporting civil rights for blacks. Likewise, the Federal Council of the Churches of Christ supported civil rights and ending segregation. The support of these denominations encouraged people, both black and white, to take a stand for equality.

In 1954, Dr. Martin Luther King Jr. (1929–1968) became pastor of the Dexter Baptist Church in Montgomery, Alabama. The following year he was elected head of the Montgomery Improvement Association, an organization created to oversee the Montgomery bus boycott in the wake of the arrest of Rosa Parks.

King became a key figure and the face of the civil rights movement. He admired Gandhi's (1869–1948) effort in India and insisted that his movement follow the model of nonviolent protest. A difficult standard to maintain, this approach offered the black community moral high ground when they were physically attacked by police and civilians alike.

Rosa Parks's Bus Boycott

Many blacks who lobbied for equality found strength in their Christian faith. While the movement was mostly nonviolent, they were often met with violence, arrest, and unjust treatment. When Rosa Parks wouldn't get up from her seat on the bus, it wasn't physical tiredness that caused her to stay seated but rather a tiredness toward injustice. She had been working in the civil rights movement for fifteen years at that point, with little success. But as a believer in Jesus, she put her life in the hands of the Lord and remained firm. With the bus boycott, Rosa Parks changed the course of racial equality in America.

In 1957, Martin Luther King Jr. helped launch the Southern Christian Leadership Conference (SCLC). Many other black clergy joined with him in this effort, such as Andrew Young, Fred Shuttlesworth, Wyatt Walker, Joseph Lowery, and Jesse Jackson. Founded as a Christian organization, the SCLC existed to end segregation.

Dr. Martin Luther King Jr. (1964)

As the SCLC's first president, Martin Luther King Jr. repeatedly spoke about nonviolent efforts. He pushed Christians of all races to end discrimination and racism. According to King, "The gospel is a two-way road. On the one hand, it seeks to change the souls of men, and thereby unite them with God; on the other hand, it seeks to change the environmental conditions of men, so the soul will have a chance after it is changed."[8] He saw the civil rights movement as nothing more than fulfilling the work of that second hand.

Another great civil rights leader, writer, and teacher was Maya Angelou (1928–2014). She said, "If God loves me. . .what is it I can't do?"[9] Sexually abused at a young age, Maya turned to literature and writing as a way of escaping the pain. In her later years, she was the coordinator of the SCLC, working with Malcolm X (1925–1965), Martin Luther King Jr., King's wife, Coretta (1927–2006), and Nelson Mandela (1918–2013).

Segregation Precedents

In *Plessy v. Ferguson*, Plessy intentionally chose to sit in a white train car as a passive protest against segregation, specifically as stated in the Separate Car Act of 1890. His lawyers argued that the act violated the Thirteenth and Fifteenth Amendments. Nevertheless, in 1896 the Supreme Court upheld the Separate Car Act as acceptable. This decision advanced the "separate but equal" doctrine. Fifty-eight years later, the tables were turned when the Supreme Court decided that racial segregation in public schools violated the Fourteenth Amendment (*Brown v. Board of Education*).

THE IMPACT OF JESUS ON CLEAN WATER

Many regions in the world still do not have access to clean water or adequate food. People waste away without hope. Missionaries and agencies serving these areas work to alleviate the physical suffering. Although driven by the gospel, they know they cannot share the gospel when people are too hungry to hear it.

Throughout history, Christian missionaries have sought to minister to people's needs so they would be open to hearing the gospel. Jesus modeled this approach Himself, twice multiplying food so that He could feed those who came to hear Him speak. Following this example, many missionaries provide food to impoverished communities—not just to feed them, but also to tangibly show them the love inspired by Christ.

Recently, many missionary and parachurch organizations have adopted the work of installing wells in developing countries. While some communities might have access to clean water, streams, or ponds, often those water supplies are corrupted by animal waste or other factors.

The Water Project calls themselves an organization of Christ followers. They answer the need of those who say, "I am thirsty." Although an organization of Christians, they don't consider themselves a religious organization. Rather, they support both religious and secular organizations to provide sustainable water to sub-Saharan Africa. They claim, "We do this work because we are Christians. Our projects do not discriminate on the basis of race, creed, ethnic or religious backgrounds. We serve others."[10] Their mission to serve people in need reflects what Jesus told His disciples: "By this everyone will know that you are my disciples, if you love one another" (John 13:35).

A similar organization, Charity Water, has adopted the method of many other organizations to partner with local ministries in their projects. Their efforts to include local churches and workers help ensure that there is someone available to maintain the well when they leave.

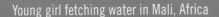

Young girl fetching water in Mali, Africa

African girl drinking clean water from a tap in Bamako, Mali

Another major player in clean water has come from former president and Southern Baptist, Jimmy Carter.

During his time as president, Jimmy Carter (born 1924) actively demonstrated his Christian convictions. Carter's Christian faith drove many of his social policies but also motivated his post-presidential work. One of the areas the Carter Center has actively worked in is the eradication of the Guinea worm in Africa.

The parasitic Guinea worm infects people who drink from stagnant water supplies that are contaminated with Guinea worm larvae. Without a known medicinal cure, the only way to get rid of the worm is to slowly pull it from a host's body over the course of weeks.

Because of Carter's convictions to demonstrate the love of Christ to the world, he authorized the Carter Foundation to work toward eradicating Guinea worm disease. To combat the problem, the Carter Foundation (and its associated

Jimmy Carter at Emory University (2008)

partners) have provided education throughout Africa and helped install clean water supplies. Over three million people suffered from the parasite in 1986, but nearly thirty years later the number of infected individuals is just over one hundred.

In general, missionary work has taken on a much more holistic approach to ministering to people, combining Christian education with ministering to their more basic needs. This holistic approach adds the gospel to the provision of food, water, education, agriculture, health care, economic projects, and construction. The process of meeting basic needs opens the doors to naturally ministering the love of Jesus Christ.

THE IMPACT OF JESUS ON MEDICAL DEVELOPMENT AND HEALTH CARE OUTREACHES

Many doctors deserve recognition for their pioneering work on the mission field, such as Dr. Paul Brand, who pioneered research into leprosy and reconstructive surgery for patients who had deformities due to the illness. Dr. Brand wrote a series of books about the connection between Christianity, faith, and medicine.

Dr. Denis Burkitt (1911–1993) served as a Presbyterian missionary and surgeon in Uganda. While treating jaw tumors in children in Uganda in the 1950s and '60s, Dr. Burkitt discovered a new type of cancer, which bears his name. He performed groundbreaking work in the use of diet to help combat cancer, based on the theory that nutrition could impact the spread of tumors. He also researched how fiber in the diet helps protect against colon cancer and other diseases.

In Africa and Central and South America, "river blindness" affects many and is caused by a parasitic worm. Medical missionary Dr. Ron Guderian discovered the source and found treatments and cures that have led to a massive reduction of this disease around the world.

Many Christian medical organizations have contributed to medical research worldwide: American Leprosy Missions, Evangelism Task Force, Fellowship of Associates of Medical Evangelism, Global Health Ministries, Heal the Nations, the Luke Society, Medical Ambassadors International, the Mercy Ships, Reach Beyond, and many others. Each contributes to medical science, with some of the best and brightest doctors choosing to serve in remote parts of the world.

State-of-the-art hospital ship (operated by Mercy Ships) serves the forgotten poor in West Africa

When the disease that would later become known as HIV/AIDS emerged in the early 1980s, there was significant public concern. Rumors and fears about how the disease might transmit to new victims fed fears inside and outside the church.

Fear drove many to react negatively toward those who were afflicted by the disease. Early reports that the disease seemed to spread by homosexual relationships led some to claim it as God's punishment on the gay community.

Yet while Christians seemed to do little to help those afflicted with AIDS in the United States, overseas Christian missionaries were active in helping AIDS victims. As the fight against AIDS has continued, Christians have

Women stand in line to get a health checkup for HIV/AIDS at a clinic in Nairobi, Kenya, Africa

been on the front lines, helping to educate people and dealing with the effects
of the disease. Franklin Graham (born
1952) of Samaritan's Purse made this
bold statement about AIDS:

Franklin Graham

> I don't care how you got AIDS—
> whether you got it from a needle,
> whether you got it through a blood
> transfusion, whether through homo-
> sexual contact, or whether just being
> careless. It doesn't matter how you
> got it. The fact is you have it. The
> church of Jesus Christ, I think, needs
> to be on the forefront of this issue, with love, with compassion, with
> understanding and giving hope to those that don't have hope.[11]

HIV and AIDS have become a bigger problem in countries where health
care is not readily available. In Uganda, the nation where AIDS originated,
the president asked for the help of the pastors and churches in battling AIDS.
The church worked with missions organizations and put into action an im-
pressive program of AIDS awareness and education.

Several missions organizations have attacked AIDS head-on, on a worldwide
basis. Organizations like Samaritan's Purse, the Salvation Army, World Vision, and Reach Beyond provide clinics and medicines to help battle AIDS.
They have worked hand in hand with local churches and Christian organizations to help educate the people in Uganda and other countries.

In the United States, Houston pastor Earl Shelp founded Interfaith Care
Partners in 1985. Working in Houston, this organization includes Christian
and Jewish congregations that provide direct support to AIDS patients and
their families. Shelp's group assigns one patient to each house of worship and
designs solutions to provide whatever support is needed.

THE IMPACT OF JESUS ON ENVIRONMENTALISM

Although environmentalism claims supporters of all faiths, some of its strongest roots grew from the active faith of Christians who aimed to protect God's
creation. The beginning of modern environmentalism may have come about
with a proposal to create "Earth Day," presented during the 1969 UNESCO

conference in San Francisco. John McConnell (1915–2012), a peace activist, is credited with making and promoting the proposal.

McConnell's concern for the environment grew out of his Christian faith. As a researcher, he established a laboratory involved in plastics production. But he was concerned about the amount of plastic waste going into the environment, plastics that were not biodegradable like most of the garbage people produce. To counter this, he sought alternative uses for the waste products.

Christians' environmental concern is based in a theology of stewardship. God has given this earth to humankind; and as such, we are responsible for caring for it. Christian environmentalists promote "creation care" and support recycling and efforts to combat global warming. In parts of the world, deforestation impacts people's daily lives and their ability to survive.

Missionaries and activists who drill wells, improve sanitation, and bring clean water to communities are doing an environmental work, which helps people live better lives.

Sewage in the streets of South Sudan

European colonialism cast one of its darkest shadows in South Africa. From the time that the first Dutch settlers arrived in 1651, colonists enslaved the tribal people living there. For over three hundred years, the black population suffered under the oppressive rule of their European masters.

In the early 1900s, the South African government offered blacks minimal rights. They were allowed to vote but not to hold office. Many laws were passed through the years, denying the black population even fundamental rights. One entire tribe, the Bantu, was disowned by the government; they were denied the right to work at even the lowest paying jobs available.

The primary church in South Africa in this time was the Dutch Reformed Church. As an organization, they were silent about the mistreatment of the black majority. That is not to say there was no Christian voice against the treatment of the blacks. As early as the 1800s, British missionaries criticized the mistreatment of blacks in South Africa. They worked tirelessly to educate and help the blacks, building churches and support systems.

Those who tried to protest the oppression many times were attacked and killed for it. What started as peaceful protests gradually became more violent as the black people found themselves ineffective in making their collective voice heard.

In the 1970s, churches and workers began to unite; blacks and whites joined in raising up their voices against apartheid. White ministers, like the Anglican bishops John Colenso (1814–1883) and Richard Ambrose Reeves (1899–1980), along with Father Trevor Huddleston (1913–1998), began spending time in black communities. The brutality inflicted on the blacks gained a witness and outspoken critic with this group of men.

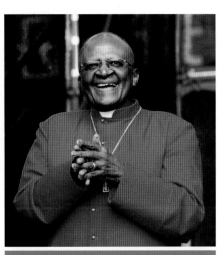

Archbishop Desmond Tutu at the "We Have Faith: Act Now for Climate Justice" Rally, Durban, South Africa (2011)

Another white minister who experienced the conditions of the blacks was Beyers Naudé (1915–2004).

He became the leading Afrikaner anti-apartheid activist. Although threatened by the World Council of Churches and his own denomination, Naudé refused to back down. Even when they revoked his minister's license, he continued fighting for the black people of South Africa. He founded the Christian Institute, which the government declared illegal. Naudé received a set of restrictions from the government, including one that forbade him from meeting with more than one person at a time.

Desmond Tutu (born 1931), a critic of apartheid, received international recognition when he became the first general secretary of the South African Council of Churches in 1978. Tutu worked to give blacks an influential voice in their own community. More black South African ministers joined in the fight—men like Manas Buthelezi, Allan Boesak, and Frank Chikane. They not only kept the fight going but also created a climate of hope among the oppressed.

Eventually, they were able to make their voice heard on an international level in the 1980s, which led to many countries around the world boycotting South African goods. This international effort severely hurt the South African economy, bringing the country to the brink of crisis. In 1991, President F. W. de Klerk (born 1936) repealed the remaining apartheid laws and called for the drafting of a new constitution.

In 1994, Nelson Mandela was elected the first president under the new constitution. Baptized and raised Methodist, Mandela also attended a church-based school. He said, "The Church was as concerned with this world as the next: I saw that virtually all of the achievements of the Africans seemed to have come about through the missionary work of the Church." [12]

Frederik de Klerk and Nelson Mandela shake hands, World Economic Forum (1992)

Prior to taking office, Mandela had spent twenty-seven years of a life sentence behind bars for his efforts to fight apartheid. While imprisoned, he was inspired by many religious organizations. The difficult lessons he had learned enabled him to emerge from prison with a message of forgiveness. His virtue allowed him to become the unifying force to forge a new nation out of the division that had existed for centuries.

The outlawing of the slave trade in Europe and the end of slavery in the United States did not end slavery on a worldwide basis. Today tens of millions of people still live as slaves. This slavery takes on many forms, including forced labor, child prostitution, adult prostitution, and even child soldiers.

Much of today's human trafficking is for the sex trade. Young women are lured into "modeling contracts" or similar false opportunities. Then their captors threaten or physically harm them to keep them in line.

In 1999, the National Association of Evangelicals, a group of twenty-eight church and parachurch organizations, launched the Initiative Against Sexual Trafficking. These groups came together for the express purpose of making a difference in today's worldwide sex trafficking and setting these slaves free.

Today's efforts to end sex slavery are widespread and often led by Christians. Christian organizations have proved especially useful at helping teens and women get off the streets and caring for the survivors.

Today, numerous Christian organizations play an active part in sex trafficking advocacy, and they work to rehabilitate those rescued from sexual slavery. The Salvation Army, World Relief, and the Christian Organizations Against Trafficking in Human Beings (COATNET) all work in this critical area. They raise awareness, act as advocates, fight the poverty and unemployment that create an atmosphere where these people can become trapped, and educate and provide assistance to victims.

Another aspect of this fight is the stand against legalizing prostitution. Some human rights advocacy groups want to legitimize prostitution, making it legal in the United States. Advocates call the practice a "victimless crime," but they hide the shame and damage to the women who live in this profession. While some women may choose to be prostitutes, many more become slaves, controlled by the pimps who use them.

> **Jesus' Impact:**
> **The Least of These Is Greatest**
>
> Jesus, knowing their thoughts, took a little child and had him stand beside him. Then he said to them, "Whoever welcomes this little child in my name welcomes me; and whoever welcomes me welcomes the one who sent me. For it is the one who is least among you all who is the greatest." (Luke 9:47–48)

As the work to free women from human sexual trafficking continues, the efforts of Christian organizations is critical. Dr. Laura Lederer (born 1951), who fought human trafficking during her tenure in the US State Department, said, "I'm convinced that faith-based communities all around the world are the only ones qualified to provide long-term care for trafficking survivors. It's the area of biggest need concerning sex trafficking, and I think it's a perfect area for the church to take leadership."[13]

Young girl working at a loom in Aït-Ben-Haddou, Morocco (2010)

QUESTIONS

1. How has shortwave radio been so effective in reaching millions of people with the teachings of Jesus?

2. In what ways were the social welfare programs established under the New Deal founded on the teachings of Jesus?

3. What kind of effort and commitment must go into the translation of the Bible into a language?

4. In what ways did some Christians follow Jesus' example by helping the Jews who were persecuted under Hitler? Why were so many churches silent in helping the Jews and speaking out against persecution during this time?

5. Why are Christian organizations often better equipped than local or federal governments in providing disaster relief to impoverished areas of the world?

6. According to the reading, "the American civil rights movement was largely a Christian movement." In what ways did Christian denominations become actively involved in the support of racial equality in the United States?

7. How have missions organizations taken on more of a "holistic approach" to ministry over the last few decades?

Afterword

HOW JESUS CHANGED THE WORLD

For 1,700 years, Christians have held a seat of power and dominated cultural decisions. With the voice of power waning, we are forced to return to Christianity in its most classical sense: to follow Jesus, to love Him with all our hearts, and to love our neighbor as ourselves.

The last fifty to one hundred years have seen a worldwide decline of the church and Christian influence. Historically strong Christian beliefs and convictions have been challenged and undermined. Behaviors once considered taboo have become mainstream.

Christians have responded to slipping influence with anger, protests, marches, and hate. These people have forgotten that Jesus did not call His disciples to win an argument—He called them to love Him and to love others. We may lose the privilege of living in a society aligned with our beliefs, but wouldn't it be better all around if we focused on preserving the true teachings of Jesus?

A RETURN TO ROOTS

Should Christians mourn the loss of their position, power, and prestige? On the contrary—the loss of power by the Christian majority around the world may urge Jesus' followers to return to the roots of following Jesus and sharing His teachings with the world. The lack of political, social, and economic power can be a painful reminder that Jesus came to set up a kingdom that is

not of this world. The loss of power may be one of the greatest blessings for the true advancement of the gospel.

Like the time of the earliest Christians, today's culture allows us to know that when people join the church, they do so out of faith, not social pressure. The scorn that often comes with following Jesus is refining and purifying. When following Jesus becomes costly, faith grows.

A FOCUS ON A TRUE HOME

Jesus was not born to grant us political freedom. In fact, Jesus Himself—and the first centuries of Christians—lived and died under the oppressive heel of the Roman Empire. It is because of this that Jesus told Pilate, "My kingdom is not of this world. If it were, my servants would fight to prevent my arrest by the Jewish leaders. But now my kingdom is from another place" (John 18:36).

Jesus called His disciples to be part of a kingdom of heaven. Being a member of the kingdom of heaven means our citizenship is not wrapped up in the things of earth, but in heaven. Consider the description of Abraham from Hebrews 11:

> By faith Abraham, when called to go to a place he would later receive as his inheritance, obeyed and went, even though he did not know where he was going. By faith he made his home in the promised land like a stranger in a foreign country; he lived in tents, as did Isaac and Jacob, who were heirs with him of the same promise. For he was looking forward to the city with foundations, whose architect and builder is God. . . .

> [Abraham and the others mentioned in Hebrews 11] were still living by faith when they died. They did not receive the things promised; they only saw them and welcomed them from a distance, admitting that they were foreigners and strangers on earth. People who say such things show that they are looking for a country of their own. If they had been thinking of the country they had left, they would have had opportunity to return. Instead, they were longing for a better country—a heavenly one. Therefore God is not ashamed to be called their God, for he has prepared a city for them. . . .

> These were all commended for their faith, yet none of them received what had been promised, since God had planned something better

for us so that only together with us would they be made perfect. (11:8–10, 13–16, 39–40)

Those who follow Jesus look forward to a kingdom that is not in this world but one where we will live face-to-face with Jesus Himself.

"Look! God's dwelling place is now among the people, and he will dwell with them. They will be his people, and God himself will be with them and be their God. 'He will wipe every tear from their eyes. There will be no more death' or mourning or crying or pain, for the old order of things has passed away." (Revelation 21:3–4)

We look forward to a life where we will be free of conflict, free of sin, and free of pain. We can look forward to a world where neighbors and friends will not make shortsighted and selfish decisions. And it will be a world where our own faith in Christ will be rewarded—we will be able to see Him and worship without hindrance. We will be able to work without thorns and continue to refine our skills and talents through eternity—all in active worship of God. That will be heaven.

And though we look forward to a pristine future, we can't forget that Jesus did not call us to build the kingdom of earth. Our hearts are not here—nor should they be. "Set your minds on things above, not on earthly things"

Christ at Emmaus, Caravaggio (1571–1610)

(Colossians 3:2). Yes, we may lose our voice in society, but that is not our ultimate concern. Our concern is to follow Christ as Lord, and to focus on loving God and loving others.

Does that mean we may lose ground in the society Christianity has built for nearly two thousand years? Perhaps that society we might prefer was never the point. Jesus did not die on the cross so that we would build an earthly paradise. He died to restore the hearts of humanity to Him. Jesus did not die so that we could win a cultural argument; He died so that we would enjoy His love and forgiveness and share these gifts with others.

A LESSON FROM ANCIENT ISRAEL

For more than one thousand years, the Hebrew people often confused the kingdom of God with the kingdom of earth. From the day God promised Abraham He would give him land, many of his descendants focused on building a lasting earthly empire rather than centering their hearts on the Giver of that land.

Sunset over the Jordan River

For centuries many Hebrews kept asking God to repel their enemies and give them physical peace, but God kept reminding them He cared about their hearts first (Isaiah 29:13). God sent prophet after prophet to remind them to turn their hearts back to Him, and He promised to use whatever means necessary to regain their hearts—including the loss of their homeland.

The promise to Abraham was never just about the land—it was about faith and relationship. For many, the land has come first, but it was never the point. If it was, the work of God would have been completed when Joshua led the people into the Promised Land. But as the book of Hebrews reminds us, God had much more in mind: "For if Joshua had given them rest, God would not have spoken later about another day" (Hebrews 4:8). God looked forward to a relationship with laws written on tender hearts rather than on civic institutions (Hebrews 10:16).

It is tempting to grow discouraged when watching our influence in culture wane, but the promise of an earthly government that acts with Christian values or a society that behaves according to our standards was never the point of Jesus, His teachings, or His resurrection.

CONCLUSION

So if Christians should have hearts in heaven, should they simply accept defeat on earth? Or should they run for office and campaign to protect children, the unborn, or families? To do anything less would not be Christian. When Christ transforms us, He changes us completely. As such, we are compelled to love, to work to improve the lives of others, and to protect the things that are important to God. Christians today have the opportunity to fight for those things—for the sake of Christ, not for that of an earthly empire.

Notes

CHAPTER 1

1. They practiced daily washing by immersion with a religious purpose.

2. If the disease was in fact smallpox, it would most likely have been an airborne illness, with the virus traveling from victim to victim by the sneezing and coughing of those afflicted.

3. Rodney Stark, *The Rise of Christianity: How the Obscure, Marginal Jesus Movement Became the Dominant Religious Force in the Western World in a Few Centuries* (San Francisco: HarperSanFrancisco, 1997), 165.

4. Lee Strobel, *The Case for the Resurrection: A First-Century Reporter Investigates the Story of the Cross.* (Grand Rapids: Zondervan, 2009), 93.

CHAPTER 3

1. L. D. Reynolds and N. G. Wilson, *Scribes and Scholars: A Guide to the Transmission of Greek and Latin Literature*, 3rd ed. (Oxford: Clarendon, 1991), 109–10.

CHAPTER 4

1 Others in the envoy included Frederick of Lorraine (later Pope Stephen IX), and Peter, archbishop of Amalfi.

2. The Eastern church was very complex. The Arabic and Oriental churches did not share the culture of the Greek church, but they all comprised the Eastern church.

3. Anselm of Canterbury, quoted in Thomas J. Kehoe, Harold E. Damerow, and Jose Marie Duvall, *Exploring Western Civilization to 1648: A Worktext for the Active Student* (Dubuque, IA: Kendall/Hunt, 1997), 323–34.

4. Alvin J. Schmidt, *How Christianity Changed the World* (Grand Rapids: Zondervan, 2004), 208.

5. Christopher Columbus, and Paul Leicester Ford. Writings of Christopher Columbus: Descriptive of the Discovery and Occupation of the New World. (New York: C. L. Webster 1892), 50.

6. "Henry VII," *Encyclopedia of World Biography*, 2004, Encyclopedia.com. July 7, 2015 <http://www.encyclopedia.com.

CHAPTER 5

1. William J. Federer, *America's God and Country: Encyclopedia of Quotations* (Coppell, TX.: Fame, 1994), 270.

2. Martin Luther, and Thomas S. Kepler, *The Table Talk of Martin Luther* (New York: World, 1952), 53.

3. The humanists of the day sought to create a society in which the citizens were able to speak and write with clarity and eloquence. This was considered necessary for

participating in the civic life of their community, as well as persuading others toward virtuous and prudent actions. Humanists studied the humanities: grammar, rhetoric, history, poetry, and moral philosophy.

4. Latin was the official language of the church.

5. Roland Bainton, *Erasmus of Christendom* (New York: Scribner, 1969), 140.

6. Tim Dowley, *Introduction to the History of Christianity* (Oxford Fortress Press, 2013), 305.

7. The Huguenots were a group of French Calvinists. They were artisans and business owners. They were not in debt to the nobility and enjoyed a level of freedom the serfs did not.

8. Dowley, *Eerdmans' Handbook to the History of Christianity* (Grand Rapids: Eerdmans, 1997), 92.

9. One notable exception is the Peasants' War in Germany. Although not directly connected to the majority of the Reformers and their work, the Reformers' words were used as a rallying cry by those promoting the war.

10. Bersier, Fondation Pasteur Eugène. "Protestant Music." Museeprotestant. org. Fondation Pasteur Eugène Bersier, October 18, 2007, accessed March 1, 2015.

11. John Calvin quoted in Alvin J. Schmidt, *How Christianity Changed the World* (Grand Rapids: Zondervan, 2004), 177.

12. "Views on Public Education by John Knox." *School Reform* accessed June 1, 2015.

CHAPTER 6

1. Charles Leslie Glenn, *The American Model of State and School. An Historical Inquiry* (New York: Bloomsbury, 2012), 32.

2. The Old Deluder Act (1647); From the Records of the Governor and Company of the Massachusetts Bay in New England (1853), 2: 203.

3. "Benjamin Franklin (1706–1790)," Benjamin Franklin Quotes. American History Central, accessed July 1, 2015.

4. William V. Wells, *The Life and Public Services of Samuel Adams: With Extracts from His Correspondence, State Papers, and Political Essays*, vol. 3 (Boston: Little, Brown, 1865), 300.

5. John Horsch, "Menno Simons' Relation to the State-Church Reformation," in *Menno Simons— His Life, Labors, and Teachings* (1916), accessed June 27, 2015 mennosimons.net.

6. Horsch, John. Menno Simons: *His Life, Labors, and Teachings* (Scottdale, PA: Mennonite House, 1916), 109.

CHAPTER 7

1. Louise Braille, quoted in Jean Roblin, *The Reading Fingers* (New York: American Foundation for the Blind, 2009), 91.

2. "Dr. Livingstone, I Presume?" http://www.christianity.com/church/church-history/timeline/1801-1900/dr-livingstone-i-presume-11630560.html (July 4, 2015).

3. "History of the Salvation Army," *The Salvation Army*, accessed July 10, 2015.

4. "William Booth Quotes," https://www.goodreads.com/author/quotes/151267.William_Booth, accessed July 4, 2015.

5. Lucy Rodgers, "Long before the Rod Was Spared." *BBC News*, May 19, 2009, accessed July 10, 2015.

CHAPTER 8

1. "HCJB Global Becomes Reach Beyond—a New Name and a New Call to Christians Worldwide," *Crossmap Christian News*, Christian News Wire, Jan 23, 2014, accessed July 6, 2015.

2. Adolf Hitler, *Hitler's Secret Conversations, 1941–1944* (New York: Farrar, Straus and Young, 1953), 6–7.

3. "About Corrie ten Boom." *Jerusalem PRAYER TEAM: About The Hiding Place*, accessed July 6, 2015.

4. F. Burton Nelson, "Pastor Bonhoeffer." October 1, 1991. Accessed July 6, 2015.

5. "Dietrich Bonhoeffer," *Christianity Today*, August 8, 2008, accessed July 6, 2015.

6. Ami Isseroff, "British Support for Jewish Restoration," *MidEastWeb*, www.mideastweb.org

7. "Video Player," Nobelprize.org, Nobel Media AB 2014, accessed July 6, 2015. <http://www.nobelprize.org/mediaplayer/index.php?id=1852>

8. "The Words and Images of Martin Luther King Jr., Malcolm X—Part 5 of 7 UNMC," University of Nebraska Medical Center. January 17, 2002, accessed July 11, 2015.

9. Maya Angelou quoted in Brownie Marie "Maya Angelou on Christian Faith: 'If God Loves Me, What Is It I Can't Do?'" *Christianity Today*, May 29, 2014, accessed July 29, 2015.

10. "Who We Are," The Water Project, www.thewaterproject.org, accessed July 6, 2015.

11. Franklin Graham, quoted in Michael Kress, "Religion in the Age of AIDS," *Religion & Ethics Newsweekly Viewer's Guide* 2003, 6.

12. Nelson Mandela, quoted in Ed Stetzer, "Nelson Mandela Has Died: Some History, Thoughts, and Reaction from South African Pastors," *The Exchange, Christianity Today*, December 25, 2013, accessed July 6, 2015.

13. Camerin Courtney, "A Q&A with Laura Lederer," *Today's Christian Woman*, 2008, accessed July 6, 2015.

Sources & Suggested Reading

Amstutz, Mark R. *Evangelicals and American Foreign Policy*. Oxford University Press, 2013.

Bonhoeffer, Dietrich. *The Cost of Discipleship*. Rev. [i.e, 2nd] and unabridged ed. New York: Macmillan, 1959.

Bowden, John. *Encyclopedia of Christianity*. New York: Oxford University Press, 2005.

Chambers, Edmund Kerchever. *The Medieval Stage*. Oxford: Clarendon, 1903.

Chester, Tim. *Good News to the Poor: Social Involvement and the Gospel*. Wheaton: Crossway, 2013.

Codex Justinianus. Macmillan, 1991.

Dowley, Tim. *Eerdmans' Handbook to the History of Christianity*. Grand Rapids: Eerdmans, 1977.

D'Souza, Dinesh. *What's So Great about Christianity*. Washington, DC: Regnery, 2007.

Ellerbe, Helen. *The Dark Side of Christian History*. San Rafael, CA.: Morningstar, 1995.

Ferguson, Everett. *Early Christians Speak: Faith and Life in the First Three Centuries*. 3rd ed. Abilene, TX: ACU [Abilene Christian University] Press, 1999.

Fox, Robin. *Pagans and Christians*. New York: Knopf, 1987.

Foxe, John, and William Byron Forbush. *Fox's Book of Martyrs: A History of the Lives, Sufferings and Triumphant Deaths of the Early Christian and the Protestant Martyrs*. Philadelphia: John C. Winston, 1926.

Glenn, Charles Leslie. *The American Model of State and School: An Historical Inquiry*. New York: Continuum, 2012.

Gonzalez, Justo L. *The Story of Christianity Volume 1*. S.l.: HarperOne, 2014.

Glenn, Charles Leslie. *The American Model of State and School an Historical Inquiry*. New York: Continuum, 2012.

Gonzalez, Justo L. *The Story of Christianity. The Early Church to the Dawn of the Reformation* Vol 1: HarperOne, 2014.

Harris, John Wesley. *Medieval Theatre in Context: An Introduction*. London: Routledge, 1992.

Kennedy, D. James, and Jerry Newcombe. *What If Jesus Had Never Been Born?* Nashville: Thomas Nelson, 1994.

Kurian, George Thomas. *The Encyclopedia of Christian Civilization*. Malden, MA: Blackwell, 2011.

Leduc, Patrick N. *Christianity and the Framers: The True Intent of the Establishment Clause*. Lynchburg, VA: Liberty University School of Law, 2011.

Ller, George, and A. E. C. Brooks. *Answers to Prayer: From George Mueller's Narratives*. Chicago: Moody, 2007.

Lockyer, Herbert. *The Man Who Changed the World: Or Conquests of Christ through the Centuries*. Grand Rapids: Zondervan, 1966.

Loeb Classical Library. Cambridge: Harvard University Press;

MacCulloch, Diarmaid. *Christianity: The First Three Thousand Years*. New York: Viking, 2010.

Mangalwadi, Vishal, and Ruth Mangalwadi. *The Legacy of William Carey: A Model for the Transformation of a Culture*. Wheaton, IL.: Crossway, 1999.

Marty, Martin E. *The Christian World: A Global History*. New York: Modern Library, 2007.

McManners, John. *The Oxford Illustrated History of Christianity*. London: Oxford, 1995.

Morris, Richard B. *Seven Who Shaped Our Destiny: The Founding Fathers as Revolutionaries*. New York: Harper & Row, 1973.

Murthy, B. Srinivasa. *Mother Teresa and India*. Long Beach, CA: Long Beach, 1983.

Schmidt, Alvin J. *How Christianity Changed the World*. Grand Rapids: Zondervan, 2004.

Shelley, Bruce L. *Church History in Plain Language*. Updated 2nd ed. Dallas: Word, 1995.

D'Souza, Dinesh. *What's So Great about Christianity*. Washington, DC: Regnery, 2007.

Stark, Rodney. *The Rise of Christianity: A Sociologist Reconsiders History*. Princeton, N.J.: Princeton University Press, 1996.

Sunshine, Glenn S. *Why You Think the Way You Do: The Story of Western Worldviews from Rome to Home*. Grand Rapids: Zondervan, 2009.

Woods, Thomas E. *How the Catholic Church Built Western Civilization*. Washington, DC: Regnery, 2005.

Zimmerman, Yvonne C. *Other Dreams of Freedom: Religion, Sex, and Human Trafficking*. Oxford: Oxford University Press, 2013.

Index

D

Rembrandt v, 126, 127
Renaissance 99, 147, 151,
153, 160
Retzius, Anders 219
Reuchlin, Johannes 151
Revelation of a Slave
Smuggler 214
Reynolds, L. D. 78, 268
Rhode Island 181
rise of Christianity 52
Rise of Christianity 26,
268
river blindness 253
Robbia, Luca della 170
Roman 2, 3, 4, 6, 7, 9, 10,
12, 13, 14, 17, 19, 20,
22, 23, 25, 26, 27, 28,
29, 31, 32, 36, 37, 39,
40, 41, 45, 48, 49, 52,
53, 54, 57, 59, 61, 62,
63, 64, 65, 69, 70, 74,
75, 78, 79, 83, 84, 85,
86, 89, 90, 94, 95, 99,
102, 104, 106, 107, 120,
130, 133, 139, 141, 147,
157, 160, 163, 165, 167,
174, 179, 208, 220, 264
Roman Catholic Church
14, 83, 120, 147, 157,
160, 167, 174, 179, 237
Roman Empire 4, 6, 9,
13, 22, 27, 32, 37, 39,
45, 48, 52, 74, 75, 78,
79, 83, 84, 86, 89, 90,
94, 95, 120, 130, 133,
139, 141
Romanesque 111, 112
Romans 2, 3, 4, 7, 18, 19,
20, 28, 29, 30, 31, 32,
37, 50, 69, 80, 133
Rome 4, 13, 14, 16, 17,
19, 25, 26, 28, 31, 37,
39, 40, 41, 46, 47, 48,
51, 52, 54, 58, 59, 61,
65, 66, 69, 70, 79, 84,
86, 89, 91, 93, 94, 98,
99, 104, 106, 107, 108,
120, 130, 138, 144
Roosevelt, Franklin D.
234, 235
Royal Institute for Blind
Youth 208
Rule of Benedict 76
Rutherford, Samuel 188

S

Sabbath 61, 106
sacraments 17, 121
Sadducees 3
Saint Helena 192
Salvation Army 221, 222,
223, 224, 230,
255, 259, 270
Samaritan's Purse 242,
243, 255
Samaritan woman 19
San Francisco 256
San Salvador 135
Sanskrit 198
Sardinia 29
sati 200, 201
Scholasticism 117, 118
school 104, 142, 146, 170,
171, 172, 173, 176, 177,
200, 208, 209, 213, 220,
225, 227, 228, 258, 269,
271, 272
schools iv, 79, 118, 171,
172, 173, 201, 228, 229,
249
science iv, 79, 83, 84, 104,
111, 116, 119, 253
Scotland 167, 168, 188,
240
scribes 87, 88, 99, 150,
268
Scriptural Knowledge
Institute for Home and
Abroad 213
sculptures 86, 127
scurvy 205
second missionary
journey 6
Seneca 78
separation of church and
state 179, 180, 181, 185
Separatists 181
Septuagint 153
sex trafficking 259, 260
sexual mores 28
Shaftesbury, Lord 227,
228, 229, 240
Shelp, Earl 255
Shipherd, John Jay 220
Shirley, Eliza 223
shortwave radio 232, 233,
261
Shuttlesworth, Fred 247

Sierra Leone 216
Silk Road 139
Simons, Menno 179, 269
Sir Edward Coke 187
Sistine Chapel 126, 127
Slave Abolition Act 192
slave boat 217
slavery 9, 10, 13, 15, 16,
17, 67, 109, 189, 191,
192, 194, 200, 214, 216,
217, 246, 259
Slavery Abolition Act of
1833 192
slaves 13, 14, 15, 16, 17,
28, 131, 188, 190, 192,
214, 216, 217, 219, 221,
259, 260
slave ship 191, 214, 217
slave trade 189, 190, 191,
192, 194, 214, 215, 216,
219, 259
Slave Trade Act of 1807
192
Slessor, Mary 207, 230
smallpox 22, 268
Social Security Act 235
social welfare 234, 235,
261
sola fide 159
sola gratia 159
sola scriptura 159
Sol Invictus 50, 59
South Africa 257, 258
South Carolina 184
Southern Christian
Leadership Conference
247
Soviet Union 241
Spain 97, 98, 112, 135,
144
stained glass 1, 77, 86,
108, 111, 112, 142, 154,
166
Staite, George 227
Stanley, Henry Morton
205, 206
stewardship 256
Stewart, Philo Penfield
220
St. Paul's Cathedral 153
Subleyras, Pierre Hubert
31
suffering 7, 12, 26, 39,
131, 132, 243, 249